(RESTRICTED) FOR OFFICIAL USE ONLY

AIR PUBLICATION 3038.
November, 1943

PAPER ECONOMY
If this copy can be dispensed with, either at once or at some future date, it should be returned to the distributing authority for transmission to the Air Ministry.

THE GERMAN AIR FORCE IN MAPS AND DIAGRAMS 1939-43

The information given in this document is not to be communicated either directly or indirectly to the Press, or to any person not holding an official position in the Forces.

NOT TO BE TAKEN INTO THE AIR

Promulgated for the information and guidance of all concerned.

By Command of the Air Council,

Published by

The Naval & Military Press Ltd
Unit 5 Riverside, Brambleside,
Bellbrook Industrial Estate,
Uckfield, East Sussex,
TN22 1QQ England

Tel: +44 (0) 1825 749494

www.naval-military-press.com
www.nmarchive.com

In reprinting in facsimile from the original, any imperfections are inevitably reproduced and the quality may fall short of modern type and cartographic standards.

THE GERMAN AIR FORCE IN MAPS AND DIAGRAMS 1939-43

	Page
PREFACE	1

I—OPERATIONAL AREAS OF COMMANDS
		Page
Map 1.	Outbreak of War, Attack on Poland (September, 1939)	3
Map 2.	End of Battle of Poland (October, 1939)	5
Map 3.	Beginning of Battle of France (May, 1940)	7
Map 4.	End of Battle of France (August, 1940)	9
Map 5.	End of Balkan Campaign (May, 1941)	11
Map 6.	Beginning of Russian Campaign (June, 1941)	13
Map 7.	Changes in the Mediterranean (January, 1942)	15
Map 8.	Summer Campaign I (May, 1942)	17
Map 9.	Summer Campaign II (June, 1942)	19
Map 10.	Summer Campaign III (August, 1942)	21
Map 11.	The Germans Driven Back (January, 1943)	23

II—ADMINISTRATIVE AND SUPPLY AREAS
Map 12.	Luftgaus in Germany, Outbreak of War (September, 1939)	25
Map 13.	Luftgaus in Extended Germany (1940-41)	27
Map 14.	Airfield Commands of a Home Luftgau (September, 1939)	29
Map 15.	An Advancing Battle-Front, France (May-July, 1940)	31
Map 16.	An Advancing Battle-Front, Russia (June-November, 1941)	33
Map 17.	A Battle-Front in Retreat, North Africa (October, 1942-March, 1943)	35

III—FLYING UNITS
Map 18.	The Varied Employment of an L.R.B. Geschwader	37
Map 19.	Moves of Short-Range Units on Russian Front (June-October, 1941)	39
Map 20.	Quick Concentration of Flying Units in the Balkans (April, 1941)	41
Map 21.	Quick Concentration of Flying Units in the Mediterranean (November, 1942)	43

IV—ARMY AND NAVAL CO-OPERATION
Diagram 22.	Army Co-operation	45
Map 23.	Naval Co-operation in the West (1942)	47

V—AIR TRANSPORT
Map 24.	Mediterranean, Rommel in Egypt (July-November, 1942)	49
Map 25.	Mediterranean, Rommel's Defeat (November-January, 1943)	51
Diagram 26.	Organisation of Air Transport	53

VI—SUPPLY AND MAINTENANCE
Diagram 27.	Provision and Maintenance of Aircraft	55
Diagram 28.	Provision of Supplies and Aircraft Equipment	57
Map 29.	Main Depots, etc. for Aircraft and Equipment (January, 1943)	59

VII SIGNALS
Diagram 30.	Signals Organisation	61

VIII—TRAINING
Diagram 31	Flying Training (1939-42)	63
Map 32.	Training units used for Air and Ground Defence (1942)	65

APPENDICES
A.	Functions of Luftflotten, Fliegerkorps and Luftgaus	66
B.	Moves of Fliegerkorps	67
C.	Functions of Airfield Commands	71
D.	Ground Organisation in North Africa (March, 1943)	72
E.	Flying Units and their Mobility	73
F.	Naval Co-operation	75
G.	Air Transport (Employment of)	76

INDEX OF MAIN SUBJECTS	Cover p. 3

PREFACE

This publication provides an outline of the activities of the G.A.F. from 1939 to 1943 by means of a series of maps and diagrams with comments. The visual method of describing the organisation and movements of Commands, ground units, and flying units has been found to be approved by a large number of Intelligence Officers. A general view of the method by which the G.A.F. has disposed its forces can be acquired in this way without unduly laborious effort. Alternatively, the publication may be used for occasional reference.

The period covered by the Maps is largely that in which the Germans were finding aggression successful. Change from success to failure means that the organisation of the G.A.F. has had to be differently applied. But it is still of practical value for us to know all the available history of the activities of the opposing Air Force.

Maps 1 to 11 illustrate the moves of the G.A.F. Operational Commands in the various campaigns; and some of these maps show the position of the G.A.F. Commands in relation to German Army Commands.

Maps 12 to 17 depict the ground organisation, especially the Luftgaue (Air Districts) and Airfield Commands both in Germany and on battle-fronts.

Maps 18 to 21 illustrate the disposition and employment of flying units, including examples of the quick concentration of flying units in unexpected emergencies.

Diagram 22 and Map 23 show (i) the organisation for Army Co-operation and (ii) the arrangements for Naval Co-operation in the West in 1942.

Maps 24 and 25 and Diagram 26 explain and provide examples of the tasks undertaken by the air transport organisation.

Diagrams 27 and 28 and Map 29 are intended to give assistance in regard to the working of the supply and maintenance system.

Diagram 30 describes the signals organisation.

Diagram 31 and Map 32 portray aspects of training in the G.A.F.

Opposite each Map and Diagram there is a descriptive Note. In some instances it has seemed that general remarks on aspects of G.A.F. organisation may usefully supplement the Notes. These general remarks, on such subjects as the functions of Commands, the moves of Fliegerkorps, Naval Co-operation, the mobility of flying units and the air transport organisation, are relegated to Appendices so as to leave the Maps as the main feature.

Information obtained from single prisoners of war has only been used when it has been possible to check it by means of captured documents, German handbooks and similar sources of information.

All the maps are on conical projection except Map 23, which is on Mercator's projection.

This publication is intended to have a circulation similar to that of A.P. 1928 (Notes on the German Air Force).

NOTE ON CONVENTIONS USED IN MAPS

In Maps 1 to 11 the basic or home areas of the Luftflotten are outlined with continuous thick lines, while the boundaries of the extended areas in occupied countries and on battle-fronts are indicated by broken thick lines. In maps such as those used, the boundaries can be only approximate. Large Arabic figures mark the areas of Luftflotten. Smaller Roman numbers mark the approximate areas in which the Fliegerkorps have operated. In instances in which Fliegerkorps have acted as independent Commands (directly under the Air Ministry) their Roman numbers have been increased in size to that of a Luftflotte figure (e.g. Fliegerkorps VIII in Map 7). Where a specially designated Command comprises a Fliegerkorps, the appropriate Fliegerkorps number is added in brackets (e.g. Command East (V)).

MAP 1

OPERATIONAL AREAS OF COMMANDS
Outbreak of War, Attack on Poland (September, 1939)

This map shows the home areas of the Luftflotten at the beginning of the War, in September, 1939.

The original Luftflotte areas were those of Luftflotten 1, 2 and 3, with headquarters at Berlin, Brunswick and Munich respectively. The fourth, with headquarters at Vienna, was added in March, 1939, after Austria and Czechoslovakia had been annexed. The district of Silesia, previously under Luftflotte 1, was then incorporated in the new Luftflotte 4.

This map also shows the position of the Fliegerdivisions (later known as Fliegerkorps) in Luftflotten 1 and 4 at the opening of the Polish campaign in September, 1939. One of the Fliegerdivisions under Luftflotte 1 (based N.E. of Berlin) supported the 4th Army attacking in a South-easterly direction. Another Fliegerdivision (based in East Prussia) supported the 3rd Army attacking Southwards. Luftflotte 4 supported the 8th, 10th, and 14th Armies attacking in an Easterly and North-easterly direction, the main strategy involving a huge pincer intended to enclose the Polish military forces in the Posen area. There were subsidiary pincers such as those which dealt with S.W. Poland, tactics which were facilitated by the use of Czechoslovakia and Silesia as starting-points. (The approximate positions of the German Armies are shown on this Map.)

It is estimated that the number of first-line operational aircraft employed by the G.A.F. in the Polish campaign was about 1,360, out of a total first-line strength of about 3,250 at that time.

It should be remarked that the Luftflotte is both an operational and an administrative Command. The two sides of its activities can be considered separately. In Maps 1-11 of this book the areas of the Luftflotten are illustrated from the operational point of view. In Maps 12-16 of the book, the areas of the Luftflotten are illustrated from the point of view of administration and supply, divided for this purpose into their constituent Luftgaus. (A short description of the functions of Luftflotte, Fliegerkorps and Luftgau is given in Appendix A.)

Under peace-time conditions each Luftflotte had a fixed establishment of flying units numbered according to a system which indicated their allegiance. This arrangement soon broke down under the stress of war, when it was found that the Fliegerkorps subordinate to Luftflotten had to have under their control such numbers and types of flying units as their tasks required at any particular time.

It should be noted that the move of a Fliegerkorps Headquarters does not imply the move of units under it. A Fliegerkorps Headquarters which is moved to a new sector may take over the units already in that sector. See Appendix B for examples of G.A.F. practice in moves of Fliegerkorps.

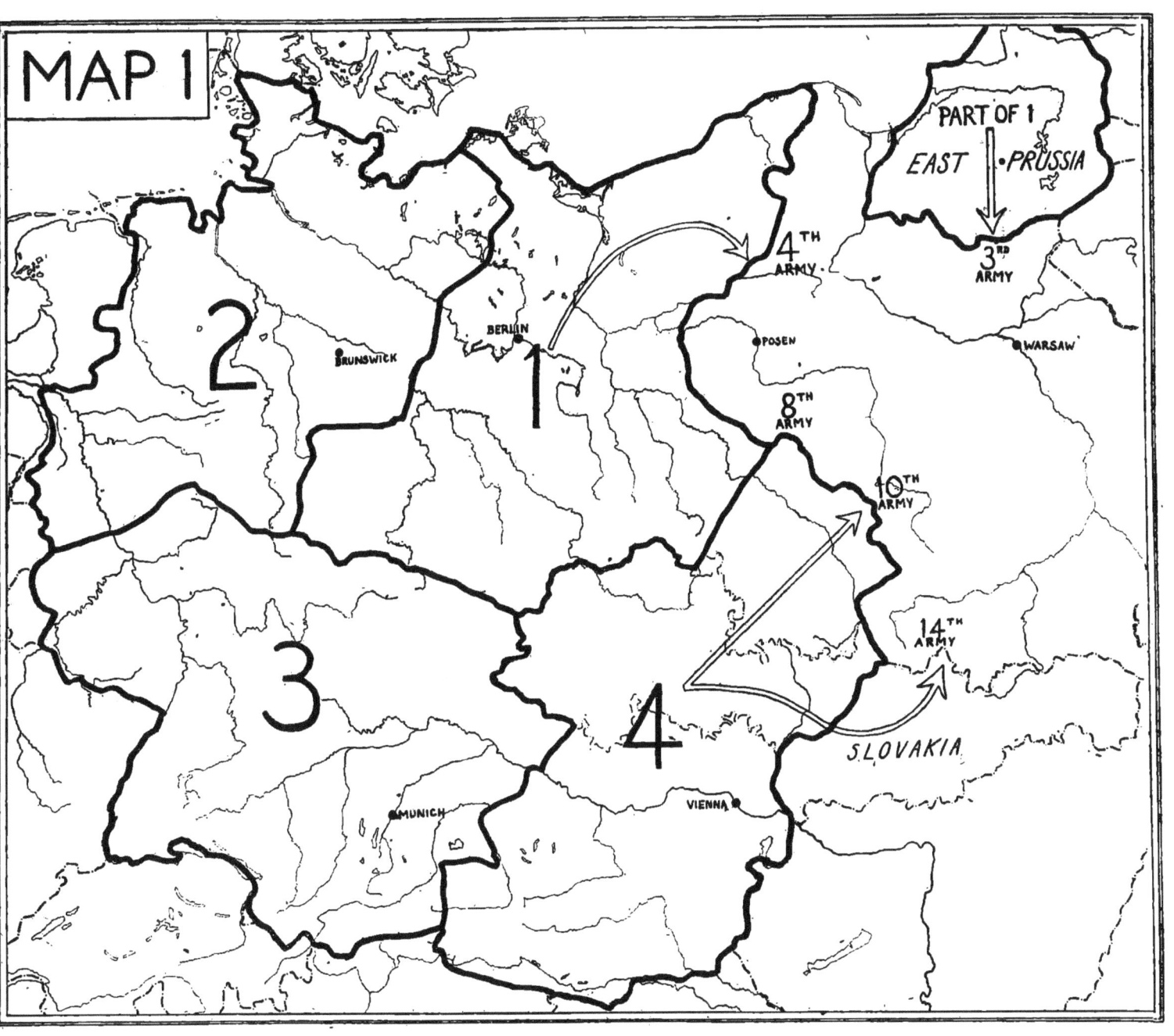

MAP 2

OPERATIONAL AREAS OF COMMANDS

End of Battle of Poland (October, 1939)

This map shows the home areas of the Luftflotten as at October, 1939, at the end of the Polish campaign and covers the period sometimes described as that of the "phoney" war. Both Luftflotte 1 and Luftflotte 4 have their home areas enlarged Eastwards into Poland—as far East as the German occupation of Poland went at that time. The home Luftgaus (administrative areas within the Luftflotten) were enlarged, and a new one established, so as to cover the newly occupied territory (see Maps 12 and 13). This arrangement was in contrast to that adopted later, in the West, where the "extended" areas of the Luftflotten (in Holland, Belgium and France) were put under the administration of new *ad hoc* "forward" Luftgaus (see Notes on Maps 4 and 15). The implication might be that it was intended by the Germans to annex West Poland permanently; whereas Holland, Belgium and France were only to be temporarily administered.

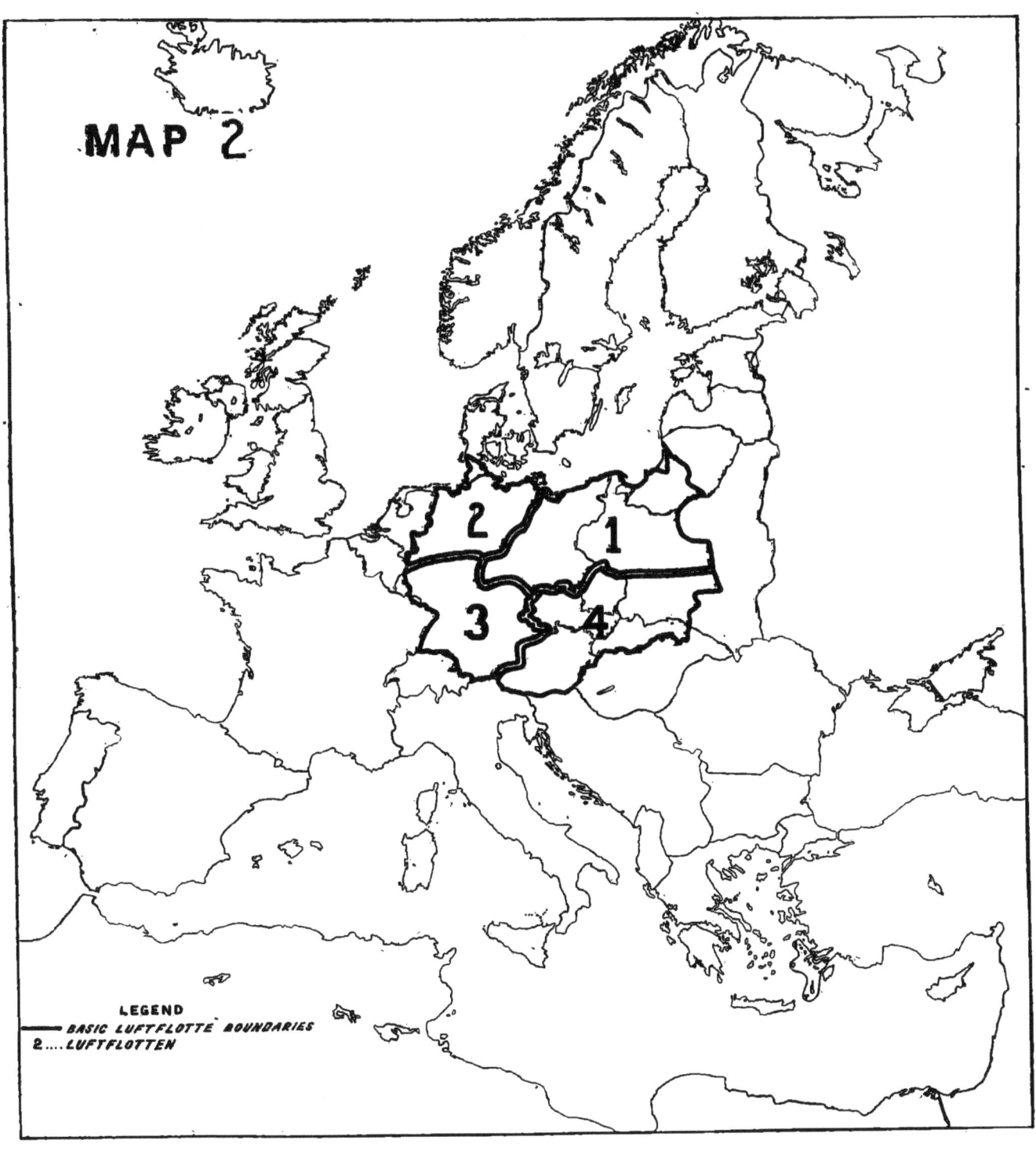

MAP 3

OPERATIONAL AREAS OF COMMANDS
Beginning of Battle of France (May, 1940)

As a result of the Norwegian campaign, in April, 1940, a new Luftflotte was created to cover Norway with headquarters at Oslo. The area of this Command (Luftflotte 5) is shown in this map, together with Fliegerkorps X which operated under Luftflotte 5 for some seven months, prior to its move to the Mediterranean. Elements of Fliegerkorps IV and Fliegerkorps I (which were in the Northern sectors in the attack in the West in May, 1940) also operated in the Norwegian campaign in April. Altogether, the maximum number of aircraft used there was about 800.

This map also shows the approximate positions of the Fliegerkorps under Luftflotten 2 and 3 at the opening of the campaign in the West, in May, 1940. Luftflotte 2 supported Army Group B (von Bock); and Luftflotte 3 supported Army Group A (von Runstedt). As stated above, Fliegerkorps IV and I were in the Northern sectors, under Luftflotte 2; and Fliegerkorps VIII, II, and V (in that order from North to South) were in the Southern sector, under Luftflotte 3.

In the first phase of the battle (10th–20th May), Fliegerkorps IV, I, VIII, II and, to a less extent, Fliegerkorps V supported the 18th, 6th, 4th, 12th and 16th Armies attacking in a Westerly direction. In the second phase (21st May–3rd June), these Fliegerkorps supported the German armies in their drive on the Channel ports. Here, in contrast to Poland, the strategy was not encirclement, but the more dangerous one, namely a huge armoured spearhead, thrust forward with great rapidity and with G.A.F. support. In the final phase (after the fall of the Channel ports), the tide of the battle turned chiefly southwards, with excursions to the Cherbourg and Brest peninsula. Fliegerkorps V which had been least active at the early part of the campaign, engaged in the bombing of Paris, and, later, operated in the area of the Aisne in the final phase of the battle.

There were about four other German Armies employed (the 9th, 2nd, 1st and 7th), in addition to those abovementioned, chiefly on the more Southern part of the front. Some of these were at first in reserve. The 1st and 7th Armies were in Army Group C (von Leeb) on the South of the line and only took a minor part in the battle.

The number of first-line operational aircraft used in *each* of the five Fliegerkorps averaged a little over 600. The total number employed in the West in May, 1940, was about 3,300 out of a total first-line strength of about 4,200 at that time. It is obvious that Luftflotten 1 and 4 had to help to provide flying units for this big concentration.

Never before, or since, has so large a number of aircraft in the G.A.F. been concentrated on so narrow a front. About 3,000 aircraft were operating in support of Armies attacking on a front of little more than 200 miles.

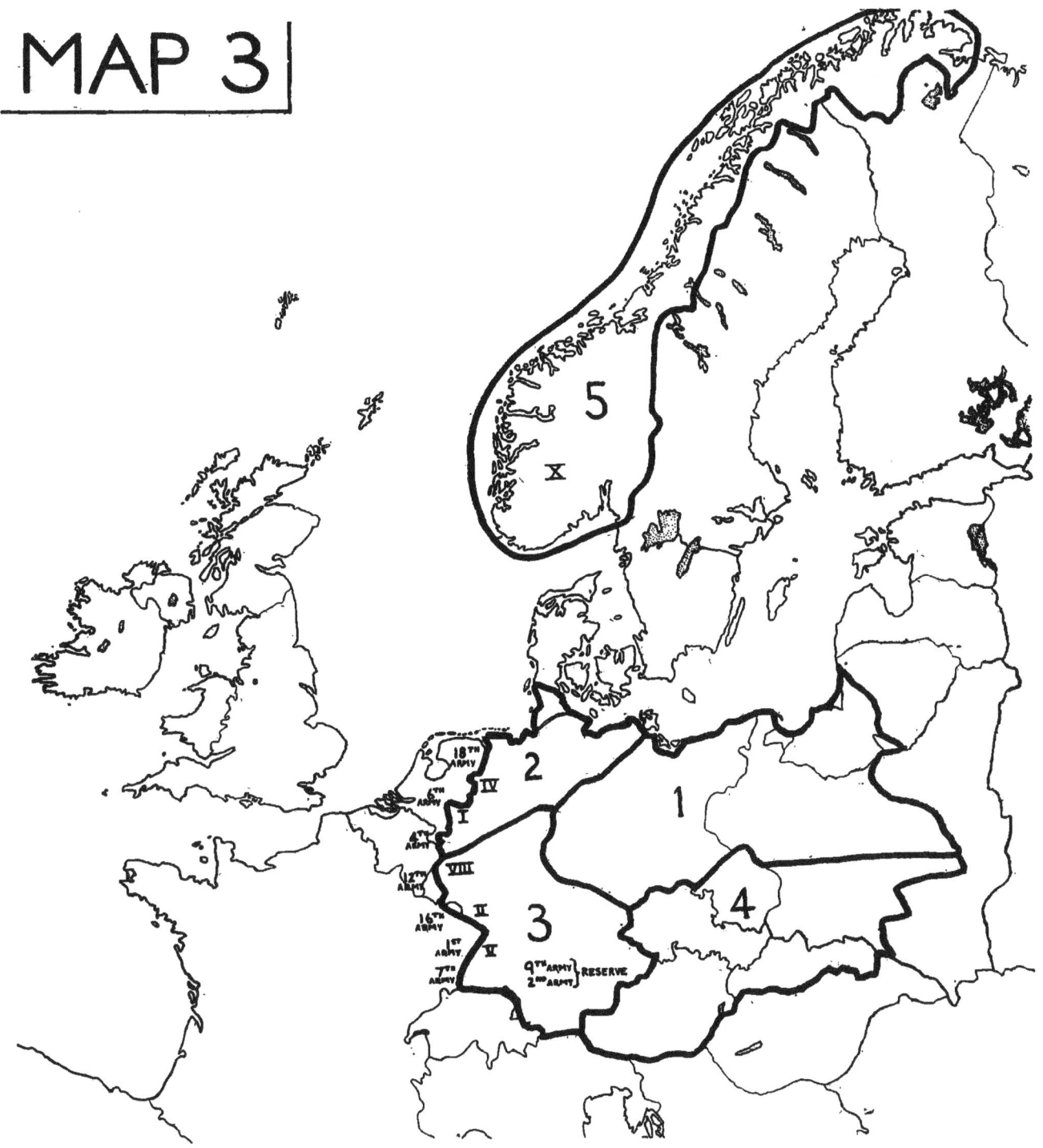

MAP 4

OPERATIONAL AREAS OF COMMANDS
End of Battle of France (August, 1940)

Apart from such an exceptional expedient as the creation of Luftflotte 5 for Norway (see Note on Map 3), it was evidently intended that invasion of neighbouring countries should be accompanied by the allocation of extended areas to the Luftflotten concerned. These extended areas would be contiguous with the home areas. In fact, it proved impracticable later in the war for this arrangement to be universally applied, chiefly owing to the need for moving a Luftflotte away from its home area to distant fronts.

This map shows the " extended " areas of Luftflotten 2 and 3 in August, 1940, at the end of the Battle of France, Luftflotte 2 in Holland, Belgium and part of North France, and Luftflotte 3 in the rest of Occupied France (see Map 11 for the later occupation of the South of France).

Fliegerkorps II occupied the most North-easterly position in Belgium and Holland, having been transferred to Luftflotte 2 from a more Southerly sector in Luftflotte 3. Next, Fliegerkorps I was based in the Northmost part of France. Both these were under Luftflotte 2.

Fliegerkorps V was based along the South of the Seine, between Paris and the mouth of the Seine. Fliegerkorps VIII was based in the Cherbourg peninsula (later a little further East) ; and it was specially engaged in operations over the Channel. Fliegerkorps IV, which had moved from the area of Luftflotte 2 to that of Luftflotte 3 (in exchange for Fliegerkorps II), was based in Brittany.

Fliegerdivision 9 (afterwards Fliegerkorps IX) operated from along the coast of Holland and Belgium. Its functions were of a specialist kind, chiefly mine-laying and attacks against shipping (see Note on Map 23).

The line of division between the sectors of the two Luftflotten ran from a point near the junction between their home areas in a Westerly direction to a little North of Paris and thence to the mouth of the Seine.

The dividing line between the two Luftflotten was further extended over the Channel and across England so as to provide sectors for purposes of bombing and reconnaissance. Luftflotte 2 operated in a sector East of a line drawn from the mouth of the Seine in a Northwesterly direction through Chichester, Oxford, Wolverhampton to Carlisle. Luftflotte 3 operated to the West of this line.

Fliegerkorps II, I, V, and IV (ranging in this order from N.E. to S.W.) were given sub-sectors ; Fliegerkorps II and I on the East of the dividing line above-mentioned and Fliegerkorps V and IV to the West of it. In the case of Fliegerkorps VIII, a sector was not allotted, as this would have been inappropriate to its activities (see above).

It was also arranged that Luftflotte 5 should have a sector of operations including Scotland and England North of a line running through Hull and Halifax.

The activities of the Fliegerkorps in the West, in the period between the end of the Battle of France and the opening of the campaign against Russia (in June, 1941), cannot be regarded as normal. Fliegerkorps are generally occupied largely in supporting Armies. But, at this period, the situation did not admit of the Armies operating, consequently, the whole of the bomber force was free to be used for strategical bombing or activities over the sea. Even those flying units, whose special work is reconnaissance for the Army, had to be diverted to short reconnaissance over the sea and nearby ports.

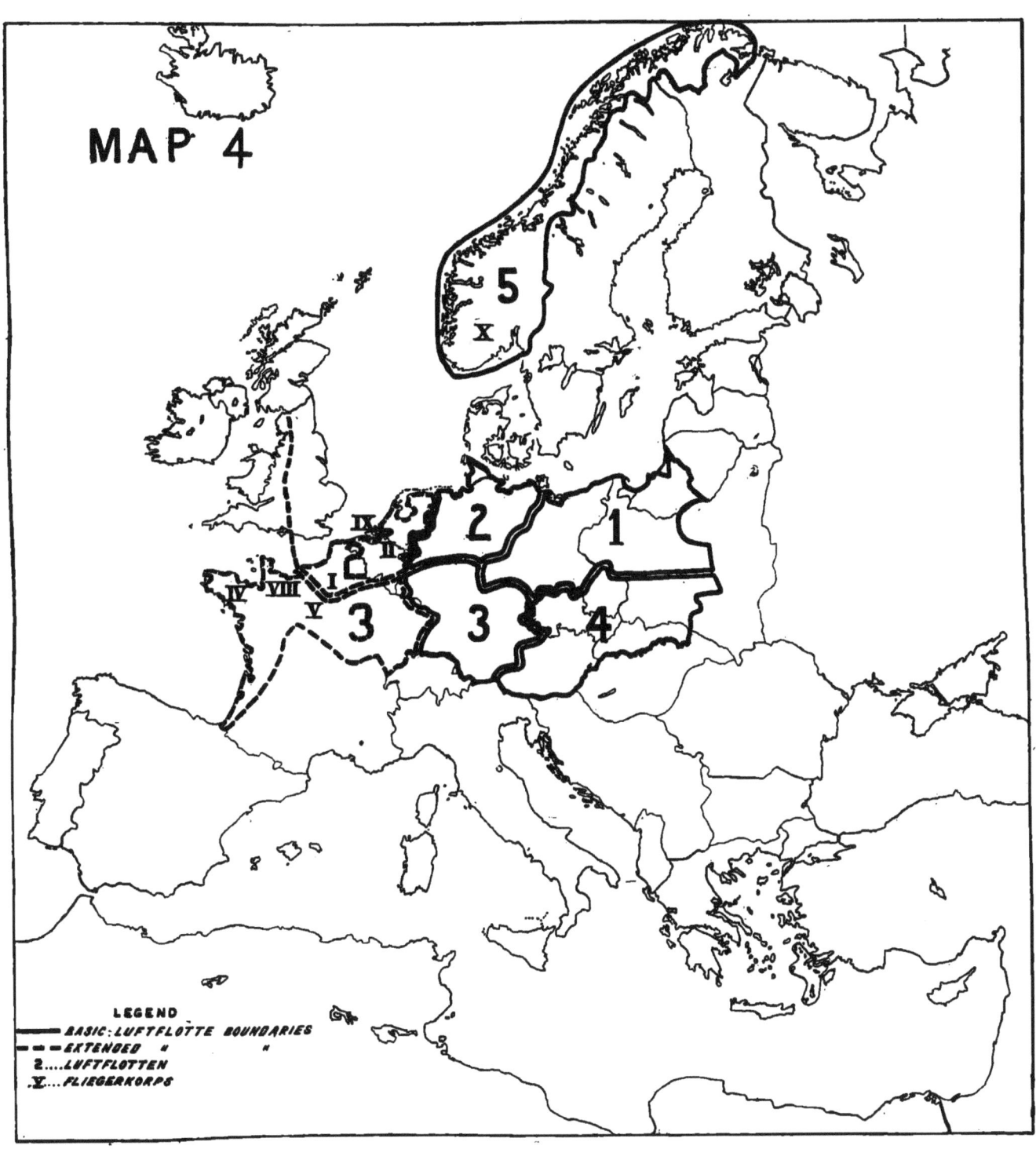

MAP 5

OPERATIONAL AREAS OF COMMANDS
End of Balkan Campaign (May, 1941)

This map shows the position as at the end of the Balkan campaign, in the spring of 1941.

By the end of 1940 the Germans had decided to send a Fliegerkorps to operate in the Central Mediterranean; and Fliegerkorps X, which had, for the preceding seven months, been operating in Norway, was chosen for this task. Luftflotte 5 was left to direct air operations in Norway without the normal intervention of a Fliegerkorps between it and the flying units. It had, however, under it two Fliegerfuehrers (later three) for controlling flying units chiefly in the North of Norway.

The area in the Central Mediterranean for which Fliegerkorps X was made responsible included South Italy, Sicily, part of Sardinia and part of North Africa. Fliegerkorps X had at this time the effective status of a Luftflotte as it operated directly under the orders of the Air Ministry.

By the middle of January, 1941, there were about 330 first-line operational aircraft based in Italy and Sicily. By March, 1941, the number was about 450, including some 200 in North Africa where a Fliegerfuehrer was established in the position, as it were, of a junior Fliegerkorps commander, owing to the detached position of the forces there. Some of the aircraft of Fliegerkorps X were used in the Balkan campaign.

Luftflotte 4, with Fliegerkorps VIII under it and also Fliegerkorps XI with Fliegerdivision 7 (parachute troops) at its disposal, was, owing to the position of its home area, chosen to control operations against Yugoslavia and Greece in April, 1941. Initially, operations were chiefly carried out by aircraft based in Bulgaria, Hungary and Southern Germany. Bases were established to the South as the campaign proceeded. (Compare Map 20.)

Luftflotte 4 is shown in this map with an extended area covering the countries overrun as a result of the Balkan campaign. The activities of the G.A.F. in this area were of a varied character, including support for the Armies attacking down the West and down the East of the Balkans, as well as operations over the sea and the landing of parachute troops together with the provision of the air support necessary for such an operation.

The number of first-line operational aircraft employed in the Balkans, Greece and Crete (exclusive of transport aircraft used for dropping parachutists or for air-landing) was at first nearly 1,000 out of a total of about 4,400 first-line operational aircraft in the G.A.F. at that time. The number was reduced in the later stages of the campaign.

The Southern boundary of the extended area of Luftflotte 2 in the West had been moved Northwards and its area reduced accordingly. Its Southern boundary at this time ran from the mouth of the Somme Eastwards, instead of from the mouth of the Seine. Luftflotte 3's extended area was correspondingly increased.

It will be seen that Fliegerkorps I has been withdrawn from Luftflotte 2 and is situated in the home area of its parent Luftflotte (i.e. Luftflotte 1) evidently making preparations for the campaign against Russia in June, 1941. It had ceased to operate on the Western Front about the end of 1940. Only Fliegerkorps II, IV and V were left in the West; and they will soon be moving Eastwards. (Fliegerkorps IX is excepted, and will remain in the West to undertake its specialised activities over the sea).

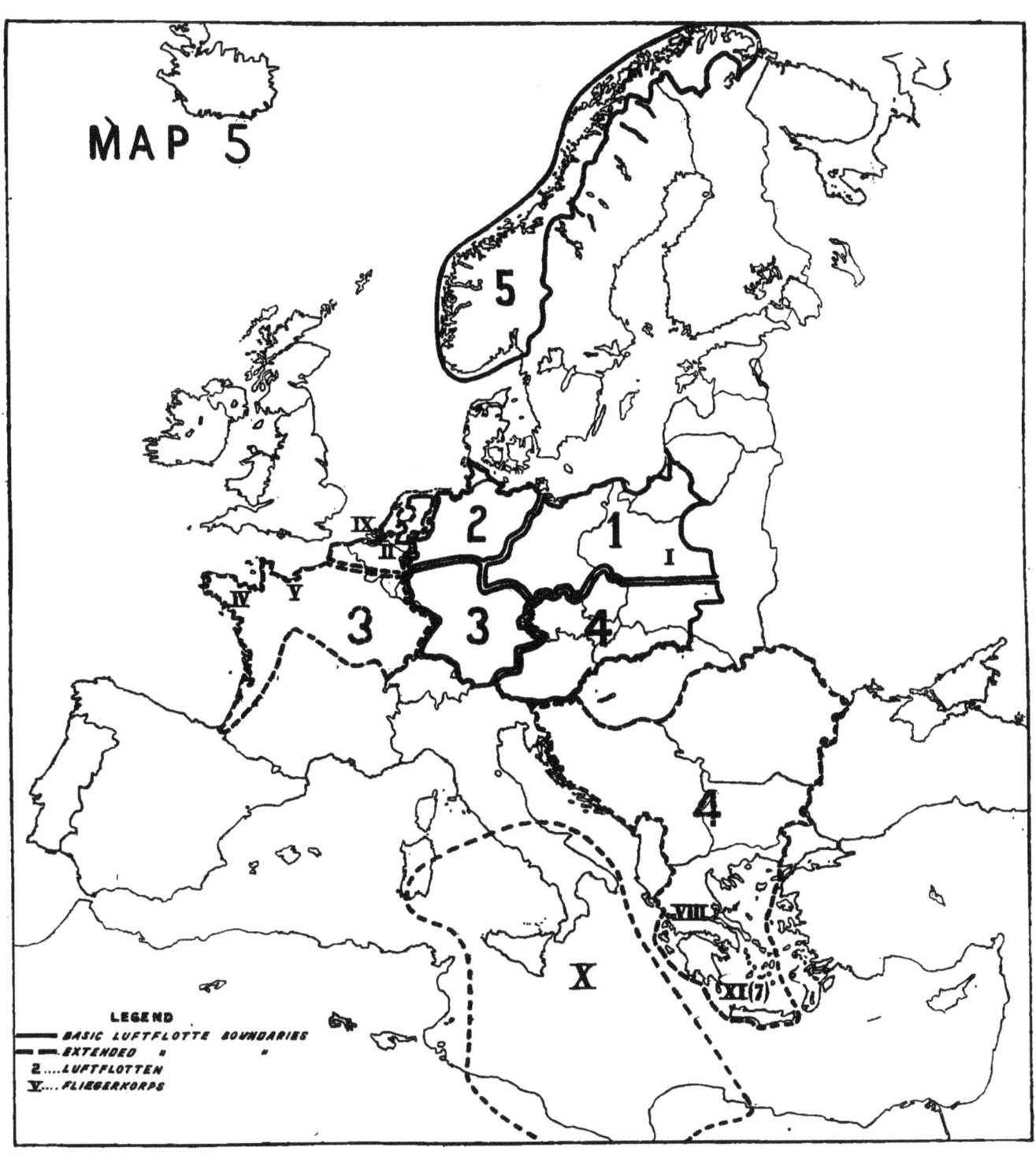

MAP 6

OPERATIONAL AREAS OF COMMANDS
Beginning of Russian Campaign (June, 1941)

At the opening of the Russian campaign in June, 1941, Luftflotten 1, 2 and 4 are ranged on the Russian front. The home area of Luftflotte 1, as enlarged in an Easterly direction after the Polish campaign in 1939, was well-placed and, doubtless, well-prepared for further extension to the East. Luftflotte 2 was introduced into the Russian front so as to reinforce it, even though this involved its being detached from its home area. Luftflotte 4, having been withdrawn from the Balkans in the previous month was given a new extended area facing East instead of South, as in the preceding campaign. As shown in the map, this sector included Rumania in the first stages of the campaign, where the G.A.F. Mission in Rumania was subordinate to it.

The sector of Luftflotte 1 looked towards Leningrad, and included the Baltic States; that of Luftflotte 2 towards Minsk and Smolensk; and that of Luftflotte 4 towards Kiev and the Black Sea, South of a line running East and West, through Lublin, including Southern Occupied Poland and Rumania. The length of front covered by these three Luftflotten was some 900 miles. (Compare Map 19.)

The number of first-line operational aircraft employed by the G.A.F. on the Russian front at the opening of this campaign was about 2,500 out of about 4,500 total first-line strength at that time. About 1,200 aircraft were left on the Western front, exclusive of Norway. The proportion of bombers to fighters on the Russian front at the beginning of the campaign as compared with that in the Battle of France is worth notice. In the earlier campaign there were 1,280 bombers and 770 single-engine fighters; while, at the opening of the Russian campaign there were 880 bombers and 680 single-engine fighters.

It will be seen that Luftflotte 1 had Fliegerkorps I under it; Luftflotte 2 had Fliegerkorps VIII and II under it; and Luftflotte 4 had Fliegerkorps V and IV under it. (Fliegerkorps VIII was transferred to Luftflotte 1 in August until September to strengthen support of the attack towards Leningrad.) The average strength in first-line operational aircraft of each of these Fliegerkorps was rather less than 500. There were also about 150 aircraft in the North of Norway and in Finland under Luftflotte 5 which should be regarded as being engaged in the Russian campaign. Luftflotte 5 is accordingly shown in this map as having an "extended" area.

The primary task of Fliegerkorps in this campaign was the support of the German Armies, either directly or indirectly. The sector of Luftflotte 1 corresponded with that of Army Group North; that of Luftflotte 2 with Army Group Centre; and that of Luftflotte 4 with Army Group South. The approximate positions of the German Armies are shown in this Map.

As a result of the withdrawal of Luftflotte 4 from the Balkans so as to occupy the Southern sector in the Russian campaign, Fliegerkorps X had its operational area extended Eastwards to cover not only the Central Mediterranean, but also Greece, Crete and the Aegean Islands. It remained directly under the control of the Air Ministry with the temporary status, though not the designation, of a Luftflotte. It had about 390 first-line operational aircraft under it, 150 of which were based in North Africa.

Luftflotte 3 is seen to be left as the only Luftflotte in the West, having to cover the area which had been previously occupied by Luftflotte 2 as well as its own. The only Fliegerkorps remaining under Luftflotte 3 was Fliegerkorps IX, whose special task is operations over the sea, e.g. mine-laying. Another specialist Command subordinate to Luftflotte 3 is Fliegerfuehrer Atlantic, whose operations are chiefly reconnaissance, covering a wide area, extending from the West Coast of France, round the Western approaches to the United Kingdom and terminating in South Norway (see Map 23). Luftflotte 3 also had under its control the O.C. Fighters who provided defensive screens down the coast from Holland to West France.

By this stage in the War, when most of the personnel of Luftflotten and Luftgau Headquarters were on the battle-fronts, it was decided to establish a new co-ordinating authority for the home Luftgaus. This amounted to, as it were, a home Luftflotte for administration and supply purposes. Its Commander was designated A.O.C.-in-C. Centre (Luftwaffenbefehlshaber Mitte). Although the original home areas of the Luftflotten remained, it is evident that from this time onwards their organisation was largely in suspense.

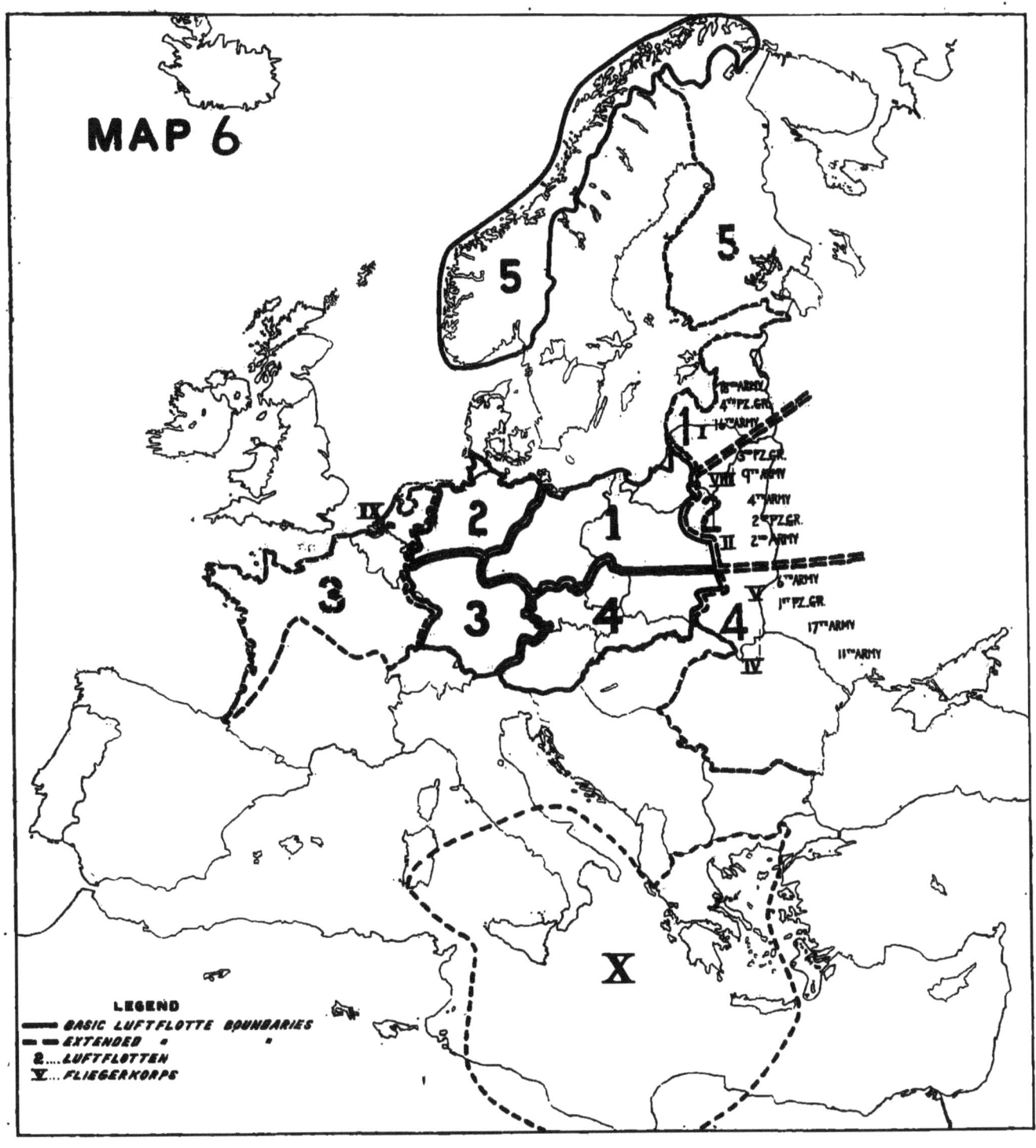

MAP 7

OPERATIONAL AREAS OF COMMANDS
Changes in the Mediterranean (January, 1942)

The changes in the positions of operational Commands which had taken place by January, 1942 were due to the decision of the Germans to strengthen their air force in the Mediterranean as a result of the British advances in North Africa.

Luftflotte 2 is seen to have moved from the central sector on the Russian front to take control of the area previously under Fliegerkorps X. Luftflotte 2 took Fliegerkorps II with it from the Russian front, and Fliegerkorps X was given the more Easterly part of the Mediterranean while Fliegerkorps II had the more Westerly. The Fliegerfuehrer in North Africa who had previously been under Fliegerkorps X now came directly under Luftflotte 2. As a result of this reorganisation, Fliegerkorps X ceased to have the effective status of a Luftflotte and resumed the status of a Fliegerkorps, becoming subordinate to Luftflotte 2.

There were at this time about 560 first-line operational aircraft under Luftflotte 2 in the Mediterranean, of which 260 were based in North Africa.

The removal of Luftflotte 2 and Fliegerkorps II from the Russian front involved readjustments there. Fliegerkorps VIII had to take over the whole of the sector which it had previously shared with Fliegerkorps II under Luftflotte 2. This sector was a very wide one to be covered by one Fliegerkorps, extending to about 400 miles, partly to the North and partly to the South of Moscow.

In view of the fact that this sector had previously been under the charge of a Luftflotte (i.e. Luftflotte 2), Fliegerkorps VIII was probably given the temporary status of a Luftflotte, in the sense that it operated under the direct orders of the Air Ministry.

At the end of 1941, Fliegerkorps V, which had been situated in the more Northerly part of the area of Luftflotte 4 (roughly speaking, the front between Kursk and Stalino) and had been engaged in support of attacks on Kharkov, was withdrawn from operations and was a little later used, in part at least, as a "Special Staff" in connection with operations in the Crimea. Fliegerkorps IV had been engaged in the autumn in the Germans' attempts to gain access to the Crimea.

It should be noted that, by this time, Luftflotte 4's area no longer included Rumania, since the G.A.F. Mission had come under the direct charge of the Air Ministry.

The number of first-line operational aircraft on the Russian front, which had been about 2,500 at the opening of the campaign in June, 1941, was reduced in the winter of 1941/42 to about 1,725, largely owing to the seasonal re-equipment and resting of flying units. Fliegerkorps I had a relatively small force of about 205 aircraft. Fliegerkorps VIII, in view of its large and important sector (mentioned above) had a large force of some 730 aircraft. Large concentrations of Close Support aircraft were maintained on the Moscow front in the autumn of 1941. Fliegerkorps VIII had to be kept strong during the winter owing to the Russian counter-offensive. Fliegerkorps IV was also a strong Command with about 640 aircraft with a wide front to cover. About 150 aircraft under Luftflotte 5 continued to operate at the extreme North and in Finland.

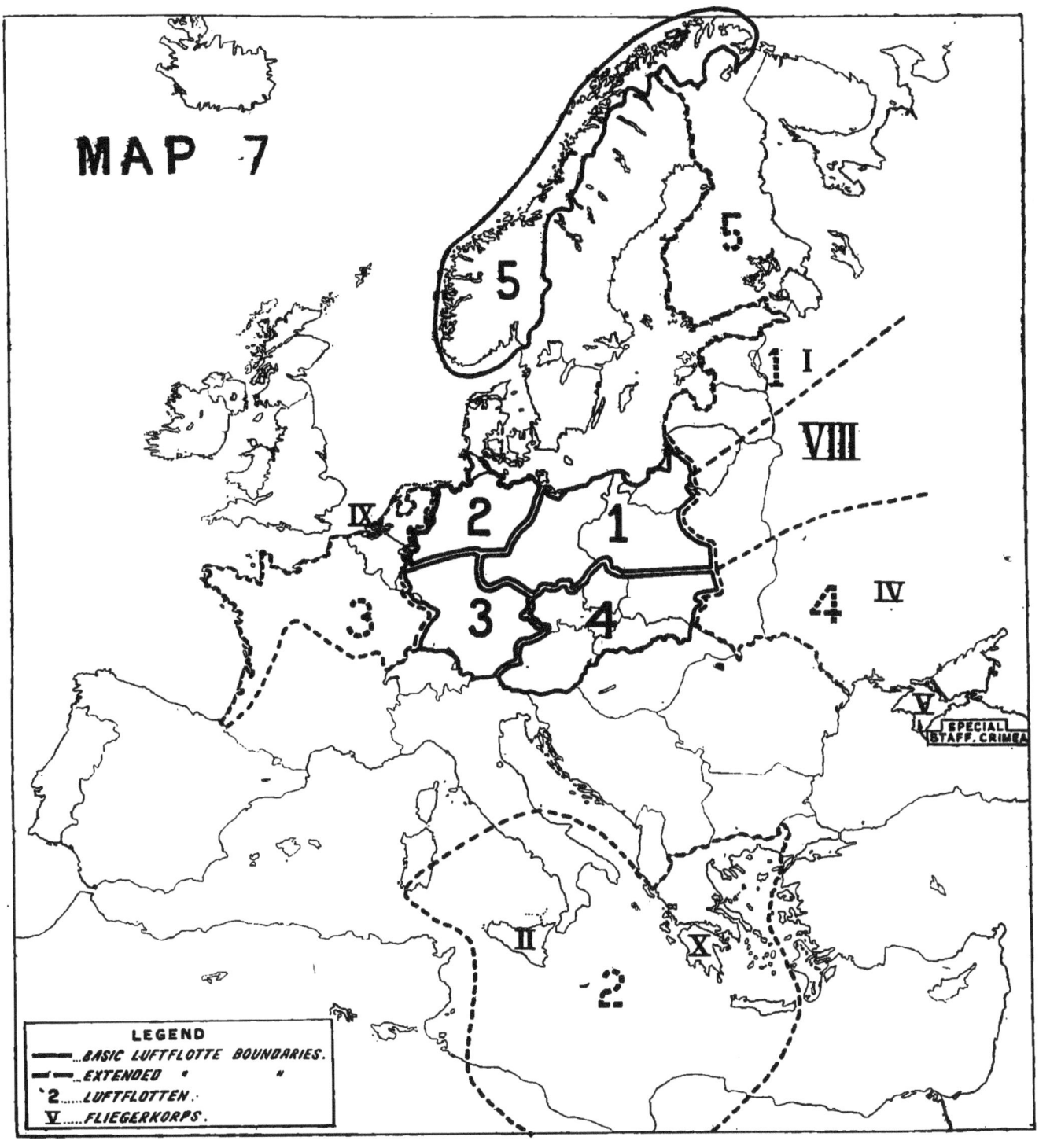

MAP 8

OPERATIONAL AREAS OF COMMANDS
Summer Campaign I (May, 1942)

By this stage in the Russian campaign operations in the Crimea were regarded by the Germans as of paramount importance, as their summer offensive against the Caucasus depended on first completing the occupation of the peninsula. Kerch had just fallen; but Sebastopol was still stubbornly resisting. Accordingly, Fliegerkorps VIII, which at this period in the War was generally selected to support the most critical operations, was moved from the Moscow front to the Crimea, coming under the orders of Luftflotte 4. The support of Fliegerkorps VIII was undoubtedly a big factor in overcoming the Russian resistance in the Kerch Peninsula.

The area vacated by Fliegerkorps VIII was taken over by Fliegerkorps V, whose designation was changed to that of "G.A.F. Command East". This Command evidently had the status of a Luftflotte and was directly under the orders of the Air Ministry. Fliegerkorps IV had had to bear the brunt of the defence against the heavy and successful Russian attacks in South Russia during March; and, in order to reinforce it, Close Support units had to be rapidly transferred from other Fliegerkorps on the Russian front.

As a result of the process of re-equipment of flying units, which had been undertaken in the winter months, the numbers of first-line operational aircraft on the Russian front had increased to about 2,300. The numbers of aircraft in the various Commands were approximately as follows:—Luftflotte 5—150; Fliegerkorps I—400; Command East (Fliegerkorps V)—500; Fliegerkorps IV—750; Fliegerkorps VIII—500.

The approximate positions of the German armies on the Russian front are shown on this Map.

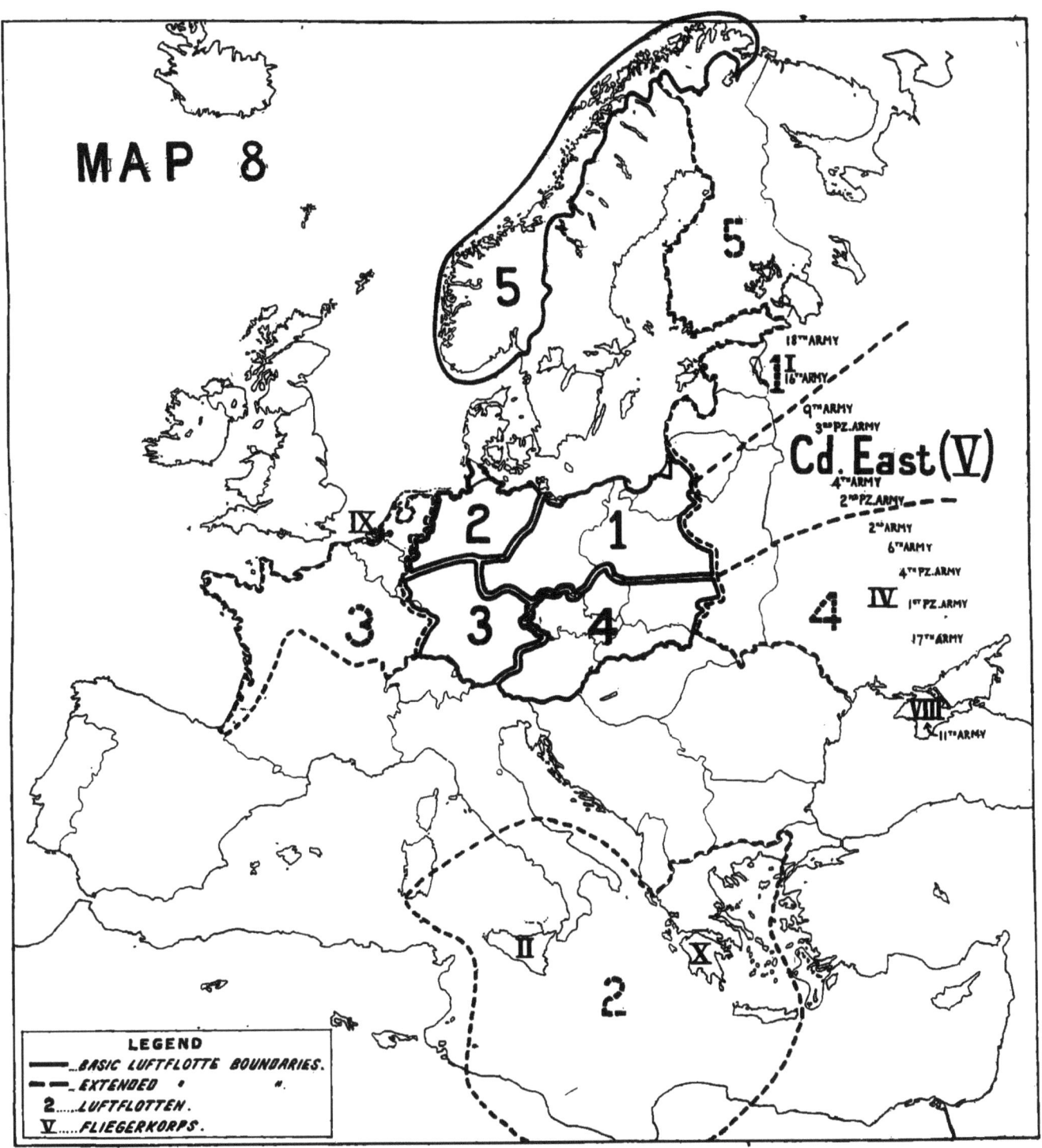

MAP 9

OPERATIONAL AREAS OF COMMANDS
Summer Campaign II (June, 1942)

The Germans were presumably satisfied that Sebastopol was about to fall. Fliegerkorps VIII could, then, be regarded as having performed its task in the extreme South of the line, and it was now moved to the new critical sector of operations. Its move was, in fact, from the Southern sector of Luftflotte 4 to the Northern sector in that Luftflotte area. This change of location took place at the period when the Germans were about to begin their new offensive on the Kursk front towards Voronezh.

As a result of the move of Fliegerkorps VIII, Fliegerkorps IV was moved to the sector abutting on to the Black Sea.

An adjustment of the area of Luftflotte 2 in the Mediterranean is shown in this map, as a result of our temporary retirement towards Alexandria.

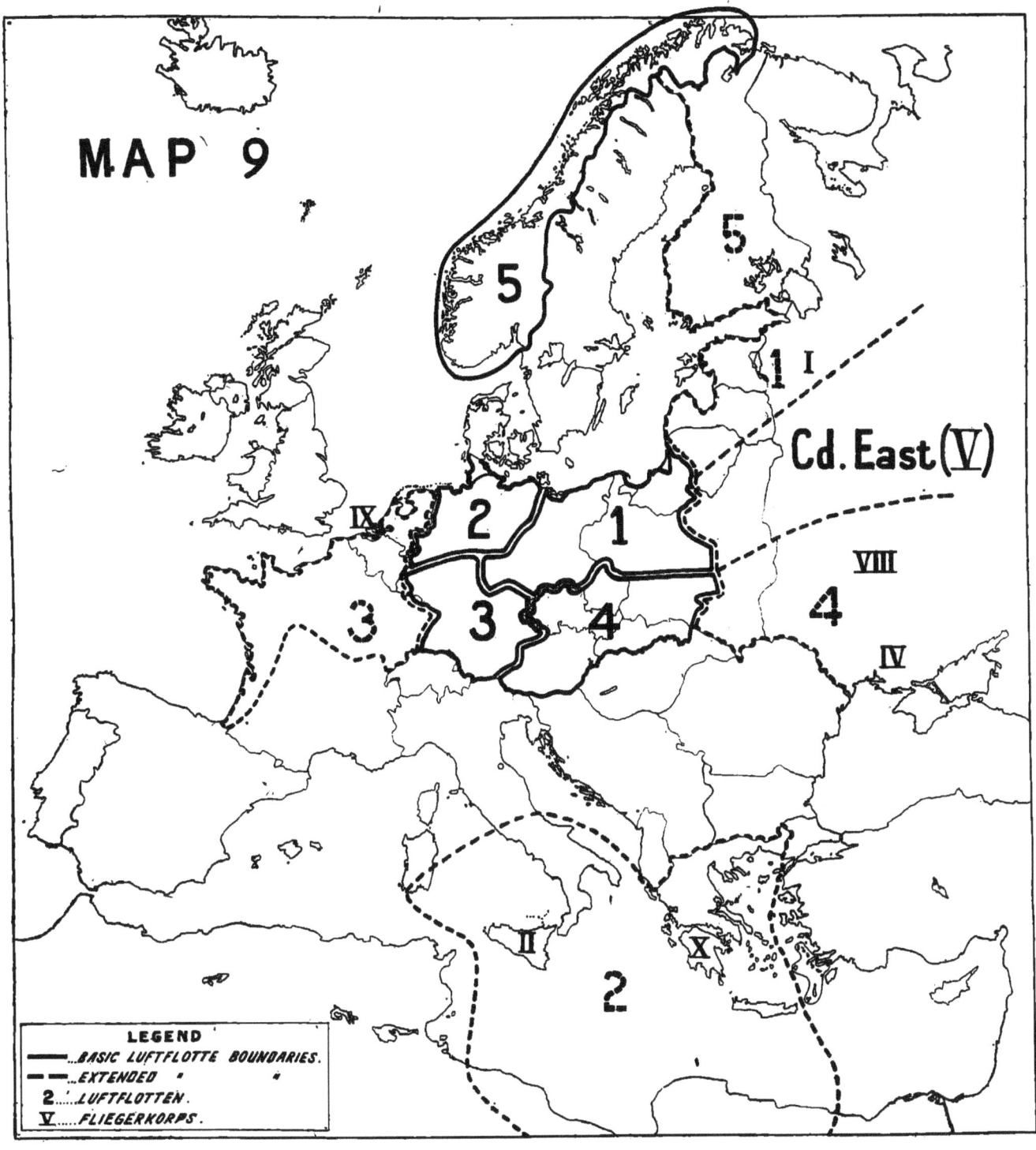

MAP 10

OPERATIONAL AREAS OF COMMANDS
Summer Campaign III (August, 1942)

In Russia, Fliegerkorps IV had, by the late summer, penetrated into the Caucasus, while Fliegerkorps VIII was charged with supporting the offensive in the Stalingrad area. Owing to the concentration of Fliegerkorps VIII's forces and to the situation in the Don Basin, it was found necessary to introduce another Command to direct operations in the North of Luftflotte 4's area, on the Voronezh front. Accordingly, Fliegerkorps I was brought down from the area of Luftflotte 1 (where it had been operating since the beginning of the campaign) and given the new designation of "G.A.F. Command Don". It presumably operated directly under the orders of the Air Ministry. Luftflotte 1 was left without any Fliegerkorps staff under it.

There had by this time been some significant changes in the numbers of aircraft employed in the various Commands operating on the Russian front. The total number of first-line operational aircraft on the Russian front had risen to 2,520, as many as those employed at the outset of the campaign. These aircraft were divided approximately as follows:—Luftflotte 5 (in the North)—250; Luftflotte 2, much reduced—180; G.A.F. Command East (Fliegerkorps V), increased—700; Command Don (Fliegerkorps I), less than 100; Fliegerkorps VIII (against Stalingrad), increased—700; Fliegerkorps IV (in the Caucasus, where the provision of air support was difficult), reduced—570; Special Command Crimea, say—60.

The approximate positions of the German Armies on the Russian front are shown on this Map.

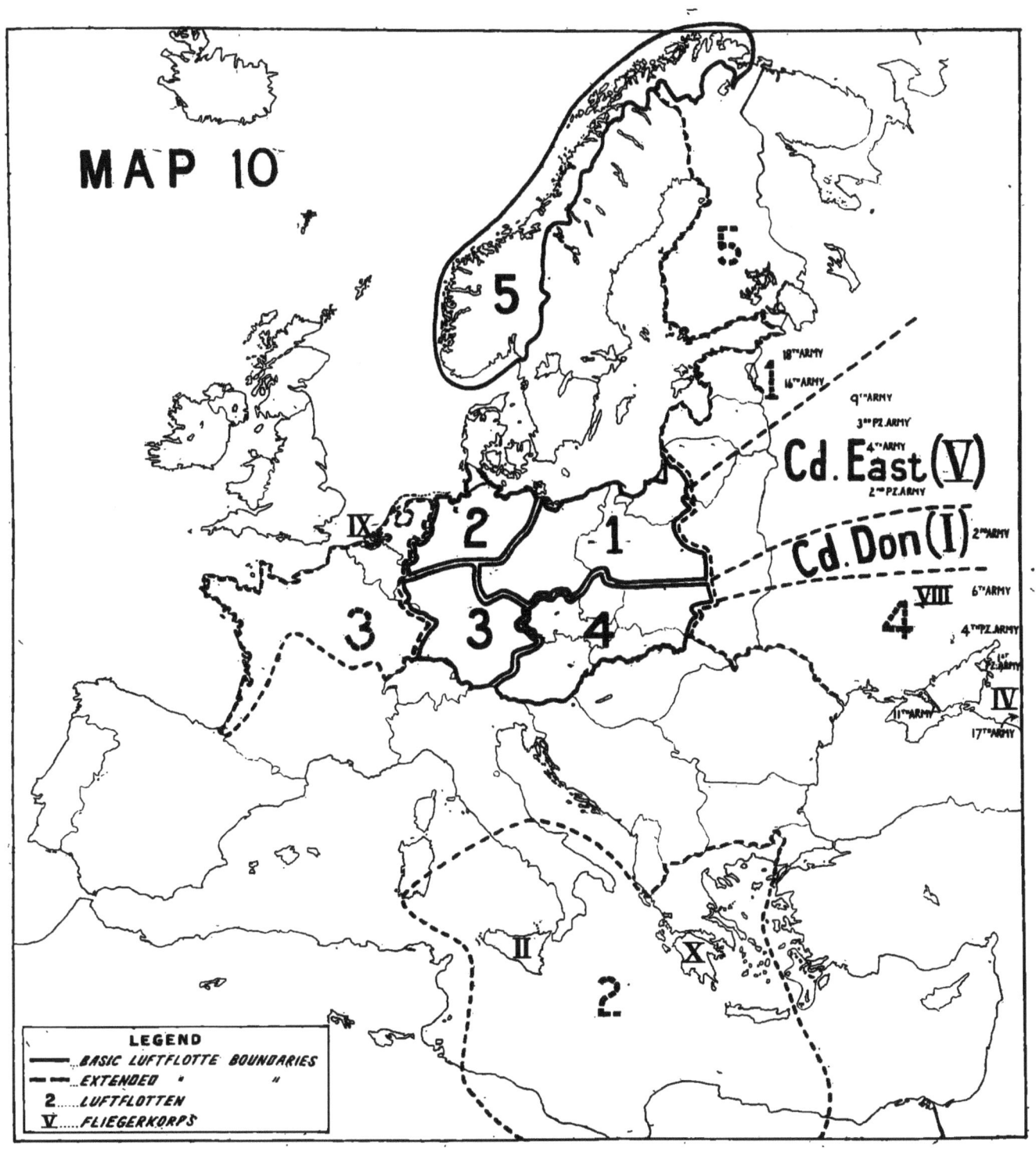

MAP 1.1

OPERATIONAL AREAS OF COMMANDS
The Germans Driven Back (January, 1943)

The relative positions of the G.A.F. Commands on the Russian front had remained unchanged since August, 1942. But the headquarters of those in the South had moved back as a result of the successful Russian counter-offensive.

The number of first-line operational aircraft on the Russian front was reduced to about 1,850, owing partly to the usual seasonal withdrawal of some flying units for re-equipment, and partly to demands for transfer of flying units to the Mediterranean as a result of the Allied activities in North Africa. The most outstanding changes in the relative strengths of the various Commands, were the reduction in numbers in Command East (Moscow front) to less than 350 aircraft, and the strengthening of the forces on the Don front to meet the Russian offensive there. Command Don (Fliegerkorps I) had been enlarged to have about 200–250 aircraft. Fliegerkorps VIII's strength was kept as high as possible to support the encircled Army. Fliegerkorps IV, which had a shorter front to cover after ejection from the Caucasus, had its numbers reduced to less than 250.

The number of aircraft in Luftflotte 1 (on the Leningrad front) remained low, though there had been a sudden, but short-lived, increase in strength there in September, 1942, probably with a view to an offensive against Leningrad which proved impracticable owing to the Russians' continued resistance at Stalingrad.

In the West the extended area of Luftflotte 3 had been further extended to cover what was previously Unoccupied France. This was the German reaction to Allied landings in North Africa in November, 1942. A new operational Command (Fliegerdivision 2), which may be described as a kind of junior Fliegerkorps, was set up in the South-east of France where the Germans rapidly concentrated for a short time over 300 aircraft, mostly from second-line and training. This number was soon considerably reduced.

At the same time the G.A.F. strengthened its position in Sardinia where a Fliegerfuehrer was established, under Luftflotte 2. The area of Luftflotte 2 is shown in the map as covering all Sardinia. It is also shown as contracted in North Africa, as a result of the Axis retreats.

By this time the G.A.F. had a maximum of 850 first-line operational aircraft in the Mediterranean, of which about 150 were in the Eastern Mediterranean under Fliegerkorps X; and a maximum of 700 were in the Western Mediterranean under Fliegerkorps II and the Fliegerfuehrers in North Africa. The numbers of aircraft on the Russian front (including North Norway) suffered some reduction in order that the forces in the Mediterranean might be reinforced.

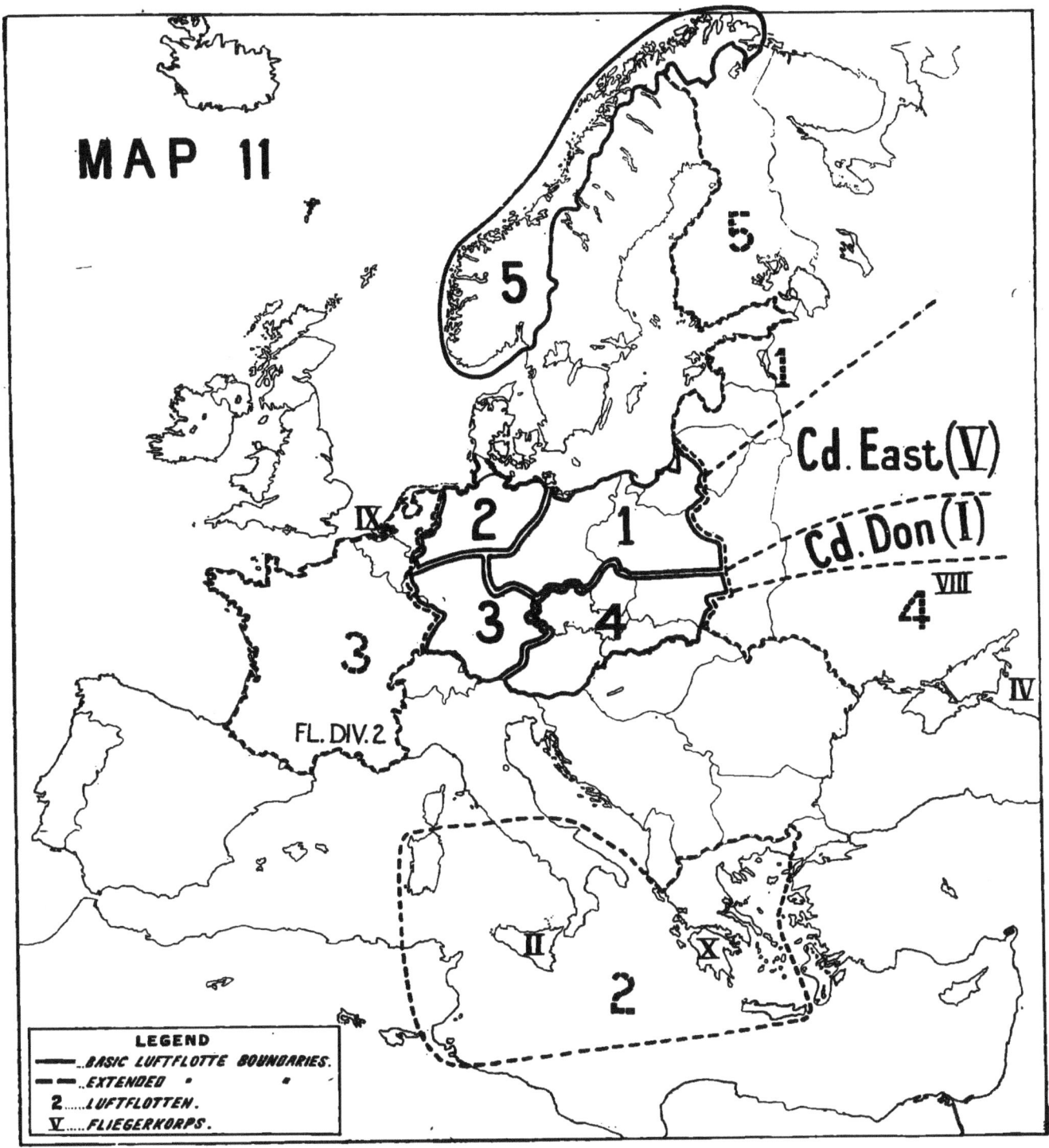

MAP 12

ADMINISTRATIVE AND SUPPLY AREAS

Luftgaus in Germany, September, 1939—Outbreak of War

As has already been remarked (Note on Map 1), the G.A.F. is divided into (i) Operational Commands and (ii) Territorial Commands for administrative and supply purposes. The Chief Commands in the G.A.F. (the Luftflotten) are both (i) and (ii). In peace-time they each have under them two or three Luftgaus (Air Districts) which are territorial Commands for administrative and supply purposes, whose business it is to look after the operational Fliegerkorps Commands. A summary of the functions of the Luftgau is given in Appendix A.

This map shows the ten Luftgaus in Germany at the outbreak of war, viz. I, III, IV, VI, VII, VIII, XI, XII, XIII and XVII. The boundaries of these Luftgaus were to a large extent based on the Army Districts (Wehrkreise) which were often smaller in size than the Luftgaus and were fifteen in number. This partly explains the gaps in the Luftgau series of numbers. For instance, some Luftgaus included two Army Districts, e.g. V and VII in Luftgau VII, and X and XI in Luftgau XI. It may be noted that the Army Commands XIV, XV, XVI and XIX were not territorial ones.

The headquarters of the various Luftgaus are shown in the map. The names of the Luftflotte headquarters are underlined. Sometimes the Luftflotte and Luftgau headquarters are in the same city.

It will be seen that the area of Luftgau I (H.Q. Koenigsberg) corresponds to that of East Prussia, and was separated from the rest of Luftflotte 1.

Luftgau XVII was formed in 1938 after the occupation of Austria.

As a result of the German entry into Bohemia in March, 1939, a new Luftflotte (Luftflotte 4) was established with headquarters in Vienna. It comprised Luftgau VIII (which had been in Luftflotte 1) and Luftgau XVII; but the Northern half of the territory of Luftgau VIII was transferred to Luftgau IV and remained in the area of Luftflotte 1.

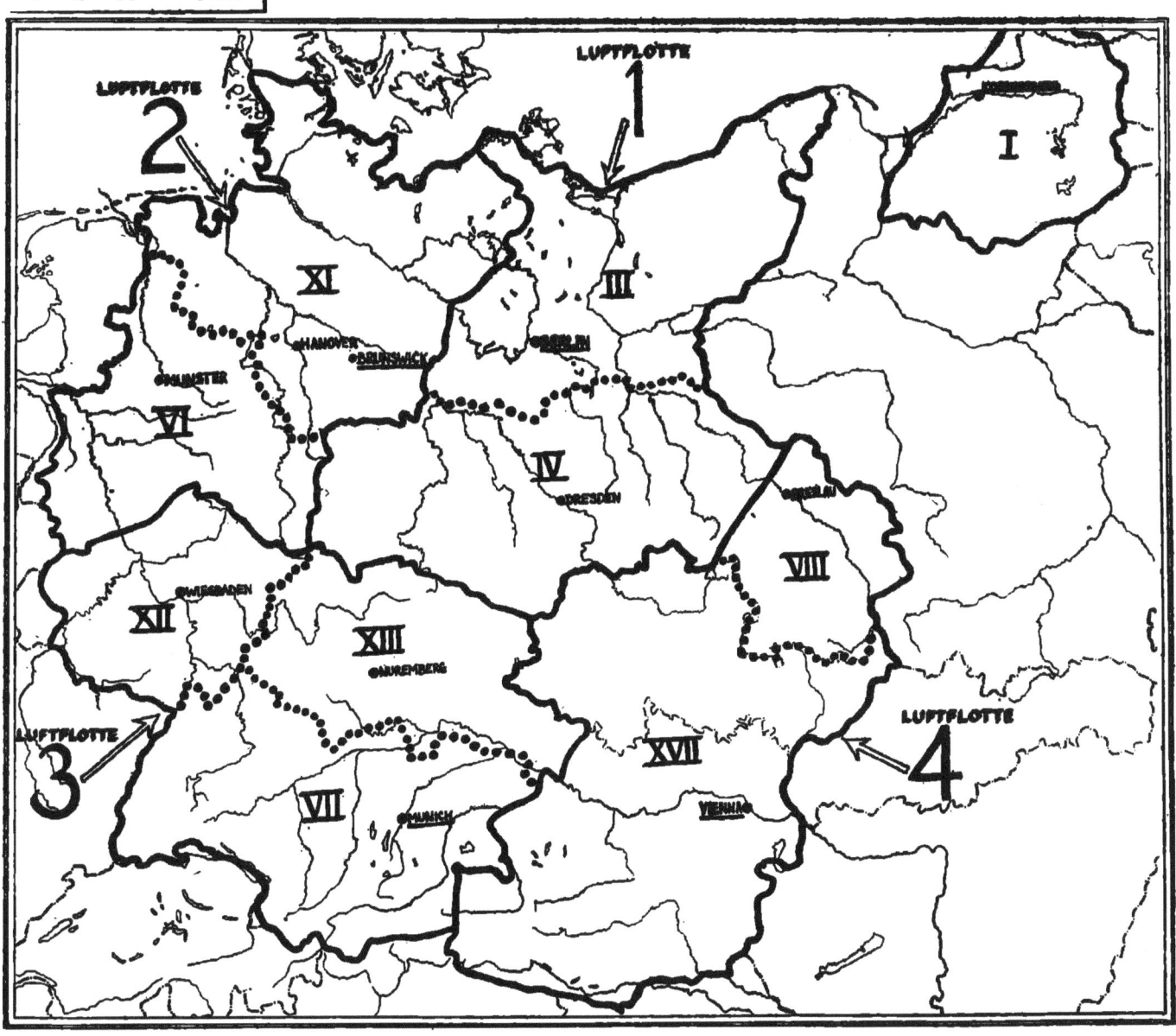

MAP 13

ADMINISTRATIVE AND SUPPLY AREAS

Luftgaus in Extended Germany, 1939-41, after the Battles of Poland and France

The chief alterations to the home Luftgau areas between the outbreak of war (see preceding Map) and the period covered by this Map are those resulting from the occupation of West Poland. Luftgau I is seen to have been enlarged to the West (to include the corridor previously dividing it from the rest of Germany) and also to the South. A new Luftgau (Luftgau II, with headquarters at Posen) was established and extended as far East as the area of occupation, as agreed with Russia. Luftgau VIII was extended Eastward to the same limit.

In the West of Europe "forward" Luftgaus for the occupied territories of Holland, Belgium and France were established, and these are described in Map 15. The implication may be that it was not the intention of the Germans to include any parts of Holland, Belgium and France in the Reich, other than Alsace and Lorraine. The procedure may be contrasted with that just mentioned in regard to Poland. But the home Luftgaus were enlarged by the incorporation into the Reich of Alsace and Lorraine, as shown in the S.W. corner of this Map.

Some adjustments were made, in the period between this Map and the last, in the areas of Luftgaus VI, XI and XII; and the site of the headquarters of Luftgau XI was changed from Hanover to Hamburg.

By 1941, administration in the home Luftgaus had become a matter of great practical difficulty since the majority of their staffs had been used for manning the "forward" Luftgaus in occupied territories (see Maps 15 and 16). Consequently certain pairs of home Luftgaus were amalgamated for most purposes, e.g. Luftgaus III and IV, also Luftgaus XII and XIII. Furthermore, the Luftflotte staffs were dispersed far and wide over Battle Headquarters in occupied countries and were no longer in Germany to control the home Luftgaus. Consequently a new Command of Luftflotte status was established (A.O.C.-in-C. Centre or Luftwaffe Befehlshaber Mitte) to control and co-ordinate the activities of the home Luftgaus, its headquarters being in Berlin.

MAP 13

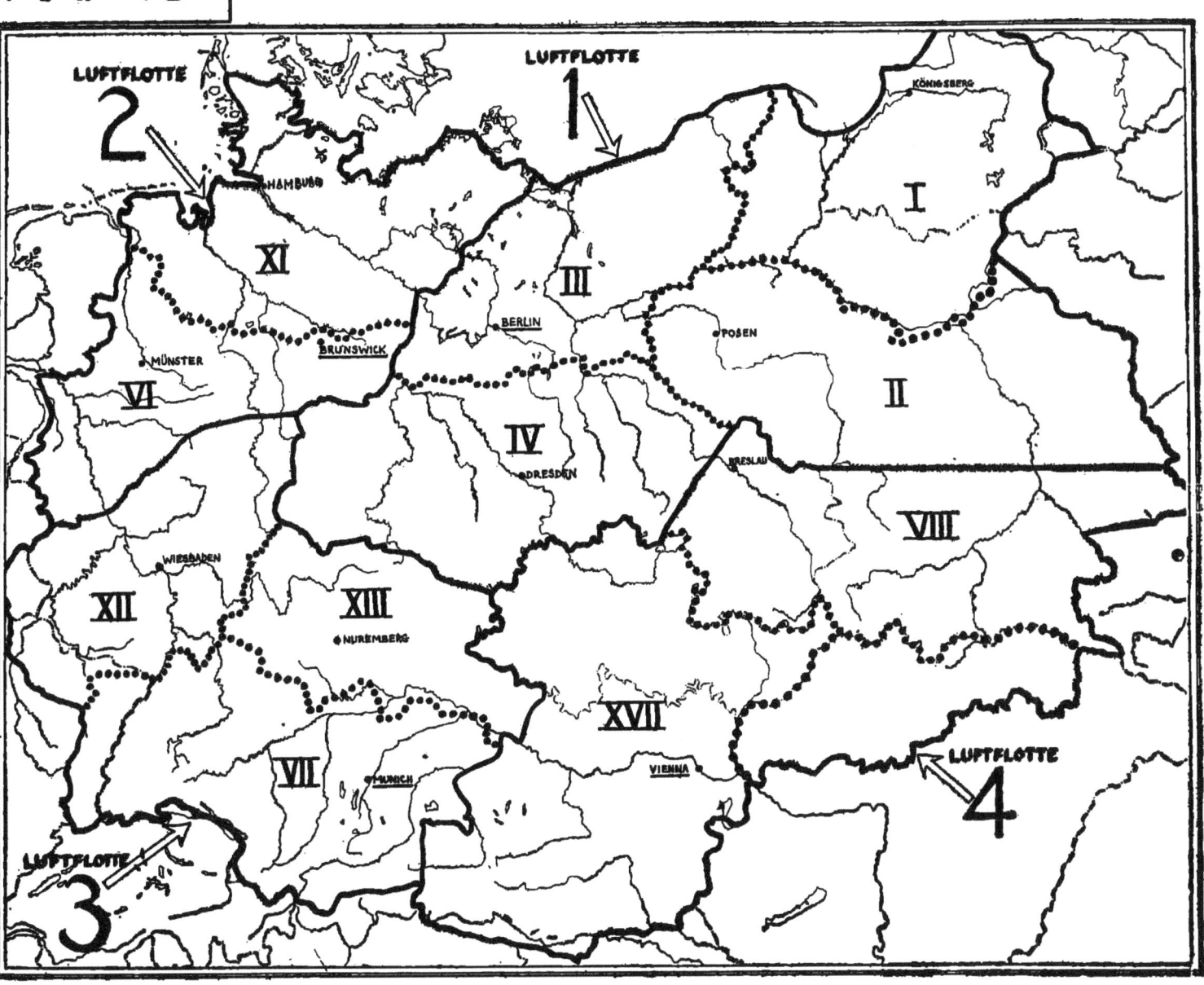

MAP 14

ADMINISTRATIVE AND SUPPLY AREAS
Airfields of a Home Luftgau (1939-40)

Luftgau VII, with headquarters at Munich, is chosen to illustrate the control of the administration and supply of airfields in Germany in 1939.

This Luftgau (like all others) is divided into regions under the charge of Airfield Regional Commands. There were six such regions in Luftgau VII, each with an Airfield Regional Command staff stationed at a selected "principal airfield" (Leithorst). These A.R.Cs. will be seen on the Map marked with the names of Böblingen, Schwäbisch Hall, Leipheim, Memmingen, Schleissheim and Aibling. Each A.R.C. had from four to seven (or even more) airfields under its supervision. (Airfields subordinate to A.R.Cs. have been frequently changed; and sometimes also the sites of A.R.C. headquarters have been altered. It is not possible to give the whole situation at any particular date.)

In the parts of Germany that are not mountainous it often happens that an A.R.C. is placed centrally to its dependent airfields, so that, looked at in map form, it suggests the anatomy of a spider. But, in Luftgau VII, this symmetrical and convenient arrangement was prevented by geographical considerations. The area is mountainous to the South and West. The best sites for airfields are, therefore, in the plain around Munich. There are only a limited number of airfield sites to the West of the Luftgau, and many of these are cut off from easy transport communication with their A.R.Cs. The area which is above the 1,200 feet contour line is shaded in the Map so as to explain in part the otherwise surprising deviation from the ideal "lay-out".

The Germans make a special point of connecting all their large airfields with the railway system. Sometimes water transport is used for transporting fuel and bombs (see below). If this Map is compared with a communications map of the same area, it will be seen that the sites of the A.R.Cs. have been chosen as being useful transport centres. Where possible the dependent airfields are situated so as to have good communication with their A.R.Cs. This has been easy in the N.E. of the Luftgau, but the configuration of the ground has sometimes prevented it in the West. (The key to the numbered airfields on the Map is given at the foot of this Note.)

In Luftgau VII, as in other Luftgaus, there is an office (largely controlled by the Director General of Equipment at the Air Ministry) called the Equipment Group. This is a misleading title because it deals with the issue not only of aircraft and aircraft equipment but also of supplies, e.g. fuel, bombs and ammunition. This office is in Munich, near the Luftgau headquarters. The headquarters of the Luftgau and the Equipment Group are often close together.

New aircraft for flying units on airfields in the Luftgau are allocated by the Air Ministry through the Luftflotte and Fliegerkorps; but the Equipment Group often has to arrange the distribution; and, in any case, has to keep records of the deliveries.

The Equipment Group also controls the issue of stocks of equipment and supplies held in main depots under its control as follows :—

(i) Aircraft equipment, kept at the Luftgau Air Park at Gablingen (No. 2 in Leipheim A.R.C. on Map).

(ii) Aircraft fuel, kept in Fuel Depots, e.g. at Freiham ("A" on Map), Weissenhorn ("B"), and Neuburg (No. 1 in Leipheim A.R.C. on Map).

(iii) Ammunition and bombs, kept in Ammunition Depots, e.g. at Kleinkötz bei Gunzburg ("C" on Map), Schierling ("D"), Schwabstadl ("E"), and Weichering ("F"). Special types of bombs may have to be obtained from outside the Luftgau.
(*N.B.*—Fuel and Ammunition Depots in home Luftgaus are nearly always sited at obscure railway stations).

(iv) Equipment and supplies for Works, kept in Works Supply Depot at Munich.

(v) Rations and clothing, kept in the Luftgau Rations Depot and the Luftgau Clothing Depot at Munich.

(vi) Medical stores, kept in the Luftgau Medical Park at Munich.

There is in the home Luftgaus some decentralisation of stocks of aircraft equipment, so that stocks are held in the A.R.Cs. Some of the heavier aircraft repair is undertaken at the "principal airfields". But at home there is less decentralisation of supplies than on battle-fronts. Most fuel, ammunition and bombs are delivered by rail or by water direct to the airfields.

A summary of the functions of A.R.Cs. is given in Appendix C.

KEY TO NUMBERS ON MAP

BÖBLINGEN A.R.C.
1. MALMSHEIM
2. NELLINGEN
3. STUTTGART/ECHTERDINGEN
4. GROSSELFINGEN
5. EUTINGEN

SCHWÄBISCH HALL A.R.C.
1. ÖDHEIM
2. DORNSTADT
3. GÖPPINGEN
4. SACHSENHEIM

LEIPHEIM A.R.C.
1. NEUBURG
2. GABLINGEN
3. AUGSBURG
4. FÜRSTENFELDBRUCK
5. LECHFELD
6. OBERPFAFFENHOFEN
7. INNSBRUCK

MEMMINGEN A.R.C.
1. LAUPHEIM
2. KAUFBEUREN
3. FRIEDRICHSHAFEN/LÖWENTHAL
4. NEUHAUSEN-OB-ECK
5. FREIBURG
6. MENGEN

SCHLEISSHEIM A.R.C.
1. INGOLSTADT
2. ERGOLDING
3. LANDAU
4. ERDING
5. POCKING

AIBLING A.R.C.
1. MUNICH/NEUBIBERG
2. MUNICH/RIEM
3. MÜHLDORF
4. AINRING
5. REICHENHALL

MAP 14

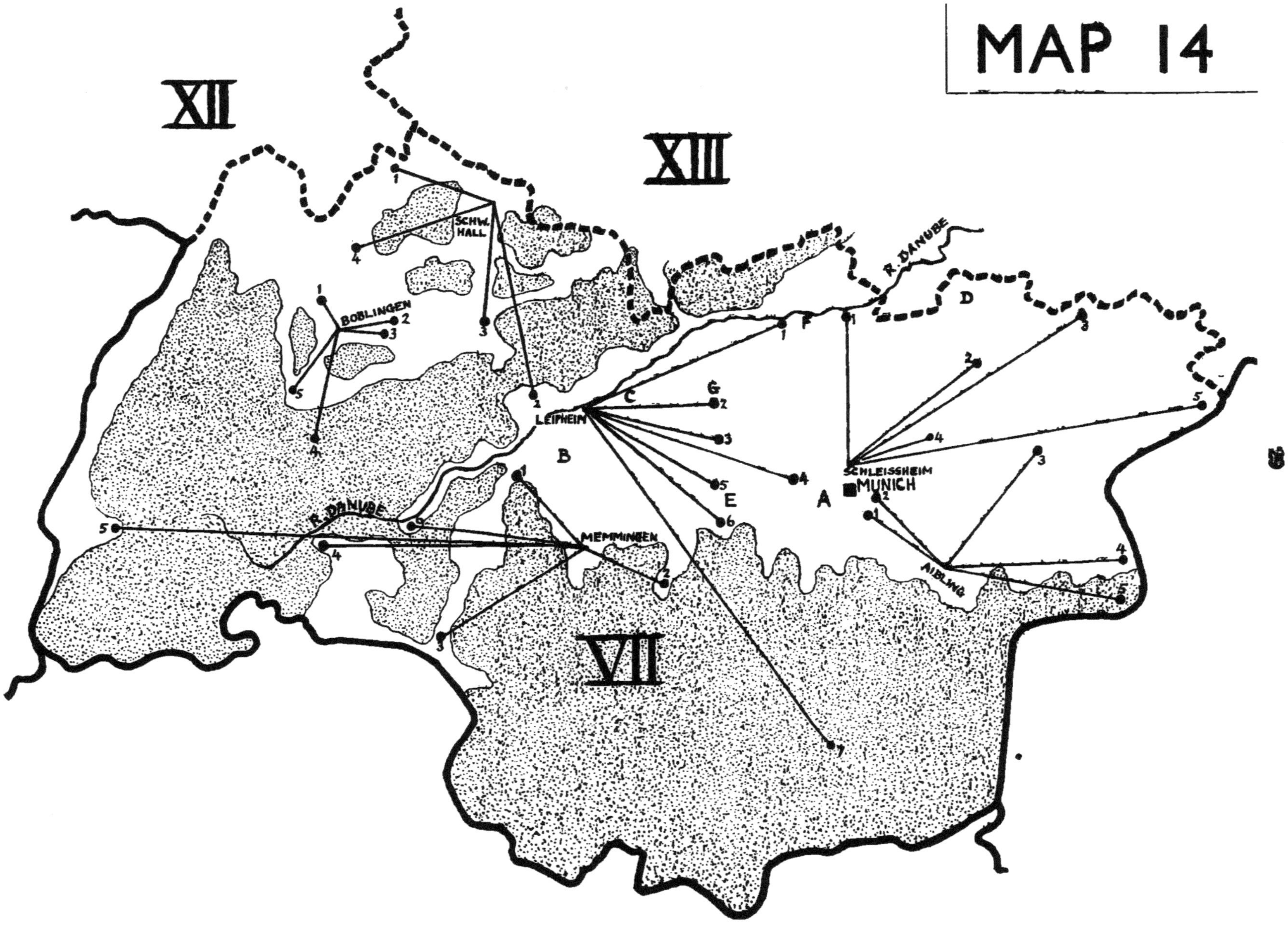
XII
XIII
VII
SCHW. HALL
BOBLINGEN
LEIPHEIM
MEMMINGEN
SCHLEISSHEIM
MUNICH
AIBLING
R. DANUBE
R. DANUBE
A
B
C
D
E
F
G

MAP 15

ADMINISTRATIVE AND SUPPLY AREAS
An Advancing Battle Front, France (May–July, 1940)

The approximate positions of the Luftflotten and Fliegerkorps at the opening of the Battle of France are shown in Map 3. The chief Luftgaus concerned in the campaign were Luftgaus XI and VI looking after Fliegerkorps IV and I (which were, at first, situated on the borders of Holland and Belgium) and Luftgau XII (and to a less extent Luftgaus VII and XIII) looking after Fliegerkorps VIII, II and V, situated, at first, on the borders of Luxemburg and N.E. France.

The G.A.F. had devised a scheme whereby special Luftgau staffs (Luftgau Stäbe z.b.V.) should be prepared prior to the offensive so as to act as spearheads of administration and supply during the expected advance. These mobile staffs were to press forward close behind the Army and were to reconnoitre and develop airfields and to improvise supplies to them in order that the flying units might give the Army the maximum support. The normal arrangement was for one special staff to be allocated to look after a Fliegerkorps.

The lines of advance of three of these special staffs, produced by Luftgau XII, are shown on this Map as the best examples available of a rapid following-up of the moving battle-front in this campaign. Special Staffs 16, 112 and 100 were formed at Wiesbaden (the headquarters of Luftgau XII) prior to the opening of the campaign. By the end of May they had reached the line St. Hubert—Charleville—Neufchateau; by early June they were on the line Guise—Soissons—Reims; and towards the end of June they had gone forward to the line Caen—Chartres—Orleans. It will be remembered that the evacuation at Dunkirk was completed by 3rd June, and Paris was entered on 14th June.

Luftgau XII sent a Battle Headquarters to Charleville as early as the end of May, and, by the end of June, this headquarters had been pushed on to Etampes (35 miles South of Paris).

Similar arrangements were made by Luftgau VI further North; but the advance had not so far to go in that area.

When, in July, the administration and supply arrangements made by the Battle Headquarters of the Luftgaus had become fairly settled, Airfield Regional Commands on the pattern of those in Germany (see Map 14) were established; and the special Luftgau staffs, having accomplished their pioneering task, were withdrawn and were either dissolved or used for other purposes.

Some of the last positions reached by the special Luftgau staffs were chosen as sites for Airfield Regional Command headquarters, which then supervised the airfields indicated by the lines radiating from Caen, Chartres and Orleans. Other Airfield Regional Commands were established further West. (For a summary of the functions of an Airfield Regional Command, see Appendix C.)

When the Battle of France was concluded, the occupied countries of Holland, Belgium and part of France were formed into three "forward" Luftgaus covering the areas shown in the Map opposite. Luftgau Holland had its headquarters at Amsterdam; Luftgau Belgium—North France at Brussels; and Luftgau West France at Etampes.

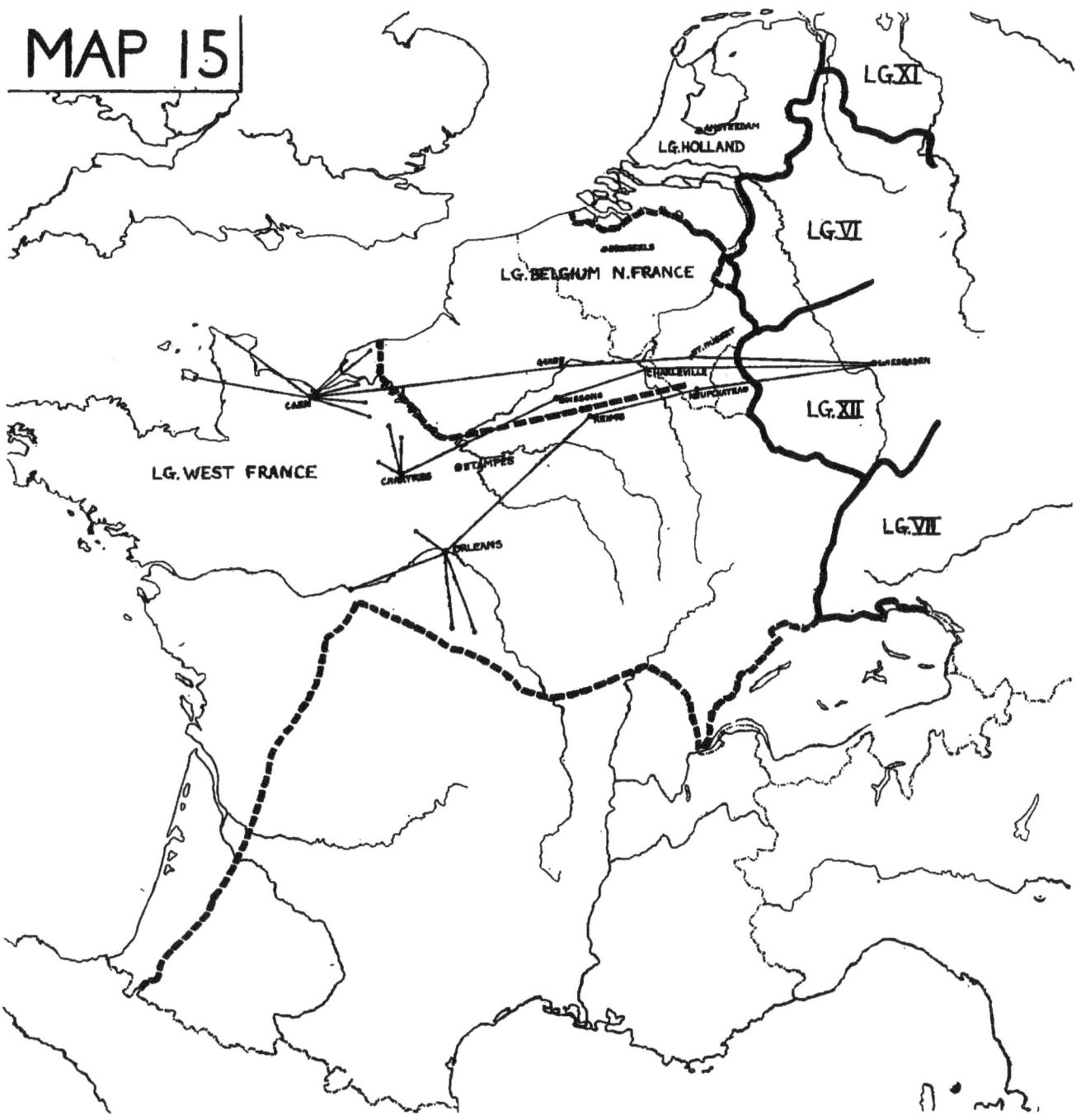

MAP 16

ADMINISTRATIVE AND SUPPLY AREAS
An Advancing Battle Front, Russia (June–November, 1941)

Special mobile Luftgau Staffs, of the same type as those used in France (see Map 15) were held ready in East Prussia and in Poland and Rumania so as to reconnoitre and develop airfields and so as to improvise supply lines for the flying units intended to push forward behind the Army in the attack on Russia in June, 1941.

In this campaign there were two of these special staffs under each of the three Luftgaus abutting on to the Russian front, i.e. Luftgaus I, II and VIII; that is to say, the general scale was one per Fliegerkorps. Special Staffs 4 and 40 were, for instance, sent forward by Luftgau VIII, No. 4 to look after Fliegerkorps V to the North of its sector, and No. 40 to look after Fliegerkorps IV to the South of its sector.

The progress of the special staffs was, as in France, close behind the Army. No. 4 reached a point 50 miles S.S.W. of Kiev by early August and was organising airfields and supplies in that area 5 or 6 weeks before Kiev was finally captured. It must have played a valuable part in forming the Southern pincer designed to close on Kiev (see Map 19).

While the special Luftgau staffs were undertaking their pioneering tasks, the three Luftgaus concerned sent forward Battle Headquarters:—

Luftgau I to Riga, in July, and later to Pskov;

Luftgau II, which was all ready with an advanced headquarters at Warsaw in June, had established Battle Headquarters at Minsk in July and at Smolensk in September;

Luftgau VIII, which was all ready with an advanced headquarters at Krakau in June, had established a Battle Headquarters at Lemberg in July.

These Battle Headquarters proceeded to organise regions to be administered by Airfield Regional Commands, so that, when a "set-up" comparable with that of the home Luftgaus was established, the special Luftgau staffs could be dissolved.

In October and in the following weeks towards the end of 1941, administration and supply arrangements in the occupied parts of East Poland and Russia had become sufficiently stabilised for a further step in organisation to be taken. The occupied area administered by the Battle Headquarters of Luftgau VIII was converted into a "forward" Luftgau under the name of Luftgau Kiev which soon set up an advanced headquarters at Kharkov. A little later, as the Germans advanced on the extreme South of the front, Luftgau VIII gave birth to a second "forward" Luftgau, which was optimistically described as Luftgau Rostov, though its headquarters were at Dniepropetrowsk except for a short time when battle headquarters were established at Rostov.

Towards the end of 1941, Luftgau II also gave birth to a "forward" Luftgau, which was likewise given an optimistic title, namely Luftgau Moscow. Its headquarters were at Smolensk.

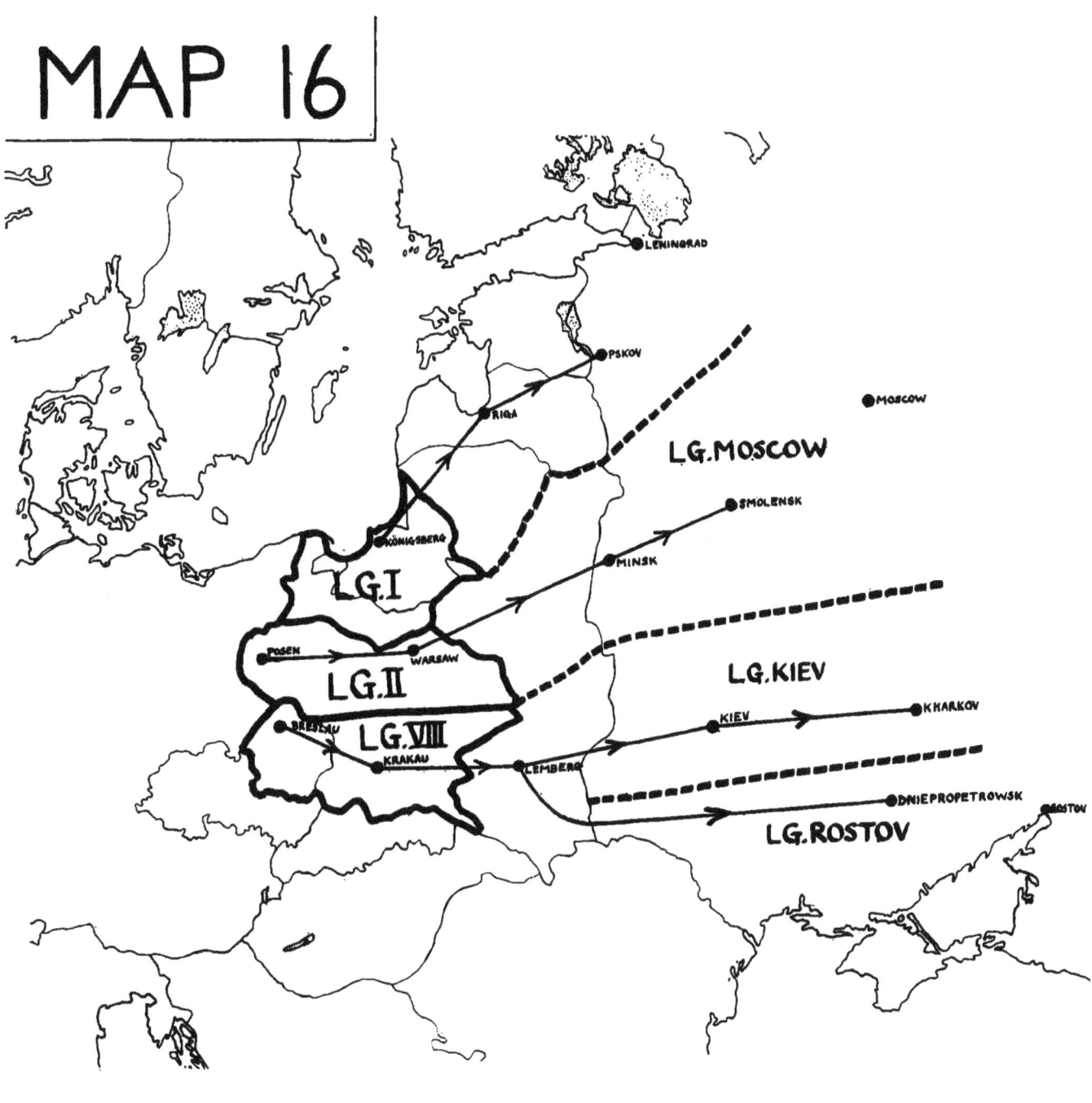

MAP 17

A BATTLE FRONT IN RETREAT, NORTH AFRICA
(October, 1942 to March, 1943)

The Eighth Army started to attack Rommel at El Alamein on 23rd October, 1942. The G.A.F. ground organisation in Cyrenaica and Egypt was divided into three Airfield Regional Commands (A.R.Cs.). A.R.C. 18/XI was in front and had charge of the airfields accommodating the short-range flying units. A.R.C. 10/III, back at Tobruk and A.R.C. 5/XIII, further back still in the Benghazi-Derna area, were largely concerned with matters of supply and maintenance, air transport, harbour protection and air escort (see Map opposite, Part I).

In the first week of November, 1942, A.R.C. 18/XI had to beat a hasty retreat and was ordered to retire to the Gulf of Sirte (the gulf S.W. of Benghazi) and do what it could to prepare the second-rate landing grounds in that area so that the G.A.F. could support Rommel in the stand which he proposed to make at the Agheila position in the Gulf of Sirte (see Map opposite, Part II).

Meanwhile the short-range flying units moved back from Egypt to Cyrenaica and were looked after for a few days by A.R.C. 10/III and A.R.C. 5/XIII. A.R.C. 10/III, when forced to retire from Tobruk on about 10th November, was ordered back to the Tripoli-Misurata area which was intended as an area for short-range aircraft supporting the Army when it should fall back to the Buerat line a little East of Misurata.

A.R.C. 5/XIII had to retire from Benghazi on about 16th November and was ordered to go right back to Tunis to organise the supply and maintenance system for the G.A.F. units which had moved to that area from Europe as a result of the Allied landings in Algeria and Morocco which started on 8th November.

A.R.C. 18/XI managed to provide sufficient accommodation for flying units on the poor airfields round Nofilia in the Gulf of Sirte to enable the G.A.F. and the Army to hold the Agheila position for three weeks (23rd November to 14th December); but the supply problem was almost a hopeless one (see Map 25); and, in spite of all efforts the number of aircraft operating at that stage fell to a low figure.

By mid-December the Eighth Army had organised Benghazi as a base, and A.R.C. 18/XI was ordered to the Sfax area which would be important for air support for Rommel when he was to hold the Mareth line and also for the covering of this area against attacks from the West which might aim at cutting off Rommel from the German forces in Tunisia (see Map opposite, Part III).

A.R.C. 10/III had a comparatively easy task when occupying the Tripoli-Misurata area. The airfields in this area were better in quality and in facilities than those near Nofilia, and the supply line was shortened. At this point, the G.A.F. helped Rommel to hold the Buerat position for over three weeks (25th December to 18th January).

A.R.C. 10/III was forced from the Tripoli area in mid-January, 1943, and was ordered to move to the Gabes area where it remained until March (see Map opposite, Part III).

It will be seen, from the description given above, that the A.R.Cs., in making their retirements, leap-frogged each other, the front one sometimes going back past two others. In this way, time was given to the "leap-frogger" to make preparations for supplies and airfield facilities, while the flying units were passing through and being accommodated by the intermediate (i.e. the "leap-frogged") A.R.Cs. This arrangement is an obvious one; but the division of the G.A.F. into two distinct branches, for operations and for supply, the latter having a territorial basis, enabled the forced withdrawal to be carried out with the minimum of disorganisation.

On the whole the serviceability of aircraft was well maintained having regard to the rapid retirement. The close-support aircraft were often engaged in fair strength in harassing attacks on the Eighth Army positions and supply columns.

Numerous documents captured in Tunisia enable a complete picture to be made of the ground organisation in North Africa as it was in March, 1943 (see Map opposite, Part III). Particulars of the various units are given in Appendix D and remarks on the functions of the various types of units are given in Appendix C. It will be seen that the A.R.Cs. had attached to them the standard sets of units:—Field Workshops and M/T Repair Platoons, Equipment Issuing Stations, Supply Stations with fuel and ammunition depots, Supply Companies, and Transport and Fuel Columns. A number of these units had travelled back from Cyrenaica, through Tripolitania with the three A.R.Cs.

In some respects the proportions of the units are not typical. The dependence on sea and air transport and the virtual absence of railway systems in Cyrenaica and Tripolitania explains this. The small number of fuel columns may be due to much of the fuel arriving in drums, which could be carried by the ordinary transport columns. The number of Works units is small, probably owing to the nature of the terrain.

It is interesting to notice how the numbering of the units indicates that, at this stage of the war, owing to the great dispersal of the G.A.F., units have been borrowed from almost every home Luftgau.

Appendix D gives, in the last three columns, details of personnel strengths, the total for the ground organisation being 8,340. The number of personnel (flying and ground) in flying units was about 2,700; Signals units 3,100; Sea and Desert Rescue 400; Fliegerfuehrer Staff 200. The total number of G.A.F. personnel in Tunisia in March, 1943, was, therefore, about 15,000.

The number of operational aircraft in Tunisia in March, 1943, was about 330, which was rather more than the number of aircraft in Egypt and Cyrenaica in October, 1942.

This Map may be usefully compared with Map 25.

N.B.—On the Map opposite, the locations of headquarters of A.R.Cs. are underlined. The airfields subordinate to an A.R.C. are ringed with a dotted line.

MAP 17

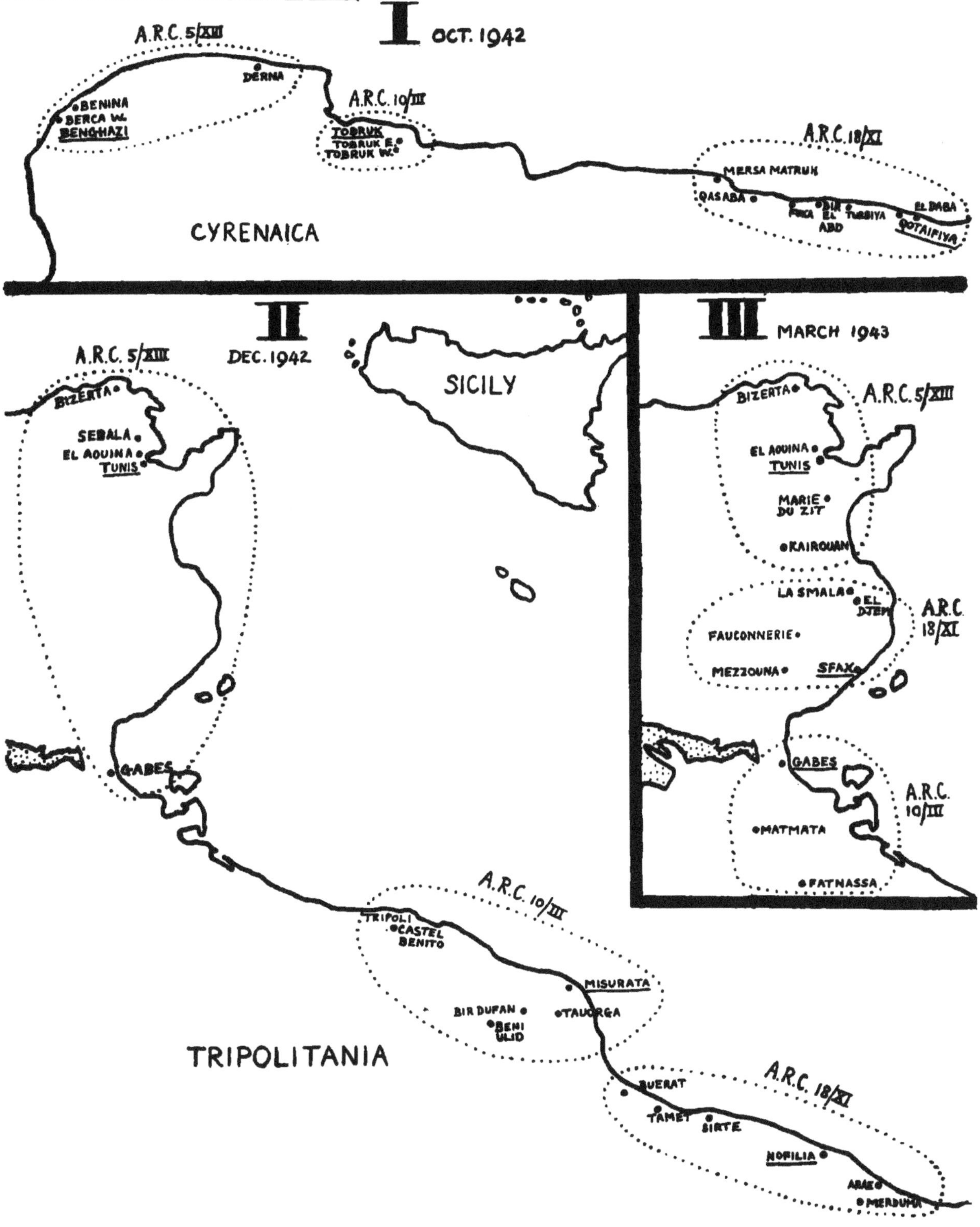

I OCT. 1942

A.R.C. 5/XIII
- BENINA
- BERCA W.
- BENGHAZI
- DERNA

A.R.C. 10/III
- TOBRUK
- TOBRUK E.
- TOBRUK W.

A.R.C. 18/XI
- MERSA MATRUH
- QASABA
- FUKA
- SIDI EL ABD
- TABBIYA
- EL DABA
- QOTAIFIYA

CYRENAICA

II DEC. 1942

A.R.C. 5/XIII
- BIZERTA
- SEBALA
- EL AOUINA
- TUNIS
- GABES

SICILY

III MARCH 1943

A.R.C. 5/XIII
- BIZERTA
- EL AOUINA
- TUNIS
- MARIE DU ZIT
- KAIROUAN

A.R.C. 18/XI
- LA SMALA
- EL DJEM
- FAUCONNERIE
- MEZZOUNA
- SFAX

A.R.C. 10/III
- GABES
- MATMATA
- FATNASSA

A.R.C. 10/III
- TRIPOLI
- CASTEL BENITO
- MISURATA
- BIR DUFAN
- BENI ULID
- TAUORGA

A.R.C. 18/XI
- BUERAT
- TAMET
- SIRTE
- NOFILIA
- ARAE
- MERDUMA

TRIPOLITANIA

MAP 18

THE VARIED EMPLOYMENT OF AN L.R.B. GESCHWADER

Among the outstanding characteristics of the long-range bomber force of the G.A.F. have been its limitation to aircraft of moderate size and the versatility of its employment. These characteristics may be illustrated by remarking on the history of a bomber Geschwader, namely K.G. 27, whose career, though very varied, is not unrepresentative.

In peace time the Geschwader was based in the Hanover area. After being employed in the Polish campaign in September, 1939, the three Gruppen moved to South Germany (Munich area) to re-equip. In March, 1940 they started to take up positions in N.W. Germany (Muenster area) preliminary to the attack on the West. After the campaign had been started a week or so (i.e. end of May, 1940), the three Gruppen moved to new bases near the Dutch frontier. Their chief activity during May was direct or indirect support of the Army, bombing such targets as troop concentrations or airfields and communications fairly close behind the line.

In the first half of June, they moved to the Lille area, in the extreme North of France, and began bombing targets in England; first airfields and, later, other targets. In the first half of July, 1940 the Gruppen moved Southwards to the Bourges—Tours area (the 3rd Gruppe moving to Rennes in August), whence strategical bombing by night was strongly sustained for the rest of the year, the main targets being ports, but other cities were also attacked.

For a few weeks in the Spring of 1941 the 1st Gruppe (using Brest as an advanced base) was given an entirely new type of activity, namely armed reconnaissance against shipping in the Bristol and St. George's Channels. In the first half of 1941, strategic bombing of targets in England continued, occasionally interspersed with attacks on airfields.

In June, 1941, the whole Geschwader was moved to Focsani (in the East of Rumania) ready for the Russian campaign. At first, the three Gruppen were employed in supporting the Army, partly by making daylight attacks on Russian airfields immediately behind the front line. In September, the Gruppen moved to Balta (inside South Russia); and, here, besides undertaking direct and indirect support of the Army, they attacked shipping at sea and in port, both by day and night. By night, they also attacked railway targets far in the rear.

In November, they moved further into South Russia, occupying airfields at Kirowograd and Cherson. At some periods between November, 1941 and April, 1942, the 1st Gruppe went back to Focsani to lay sea-mines in the Black Sea and Crimean ports; but it was also temporarily transferred to Saporoshje to deal with urgent Army requirements for support, e.g. at Perekop for the attack on the Crimea. At the same time, the 3rd Gruppe had very varied tasks, namely, sea reconnaissance, land reconnaissance, attacks on ships, and, occasionally close support of the Army. The 2nd Gruppe, after resting and refitting, had been sent for a short time, in the early part of 1942, to the Leningrad front. In the spring of 1942, all three Gruppen were reunited at Cherson.

In the Summer of 1942, two Gruppen were moved to Kharkov and later to Kursk, where they were chiefly engaged in giving support to the Army, either near the battle area or in the area behind the lines, where the targets were communications, airfields and depots. One Gruppe was detached for a time to attack shipping in the Black Sea.

It is remarkable that the units of K.G. 27, in undertaking the varied tasks outlined above, were not at any time subordinated to functional Commands, but remained under the direct control of Fliegerkorps. In 1942, however, the long-range bomber forces in South Russia were organised under the charge of an O.C. Long-Range Bombers of the Luftflotte and could be transferred from the operational area and subordination of one Fliegerkorps in the Luftflotte to another according to need.

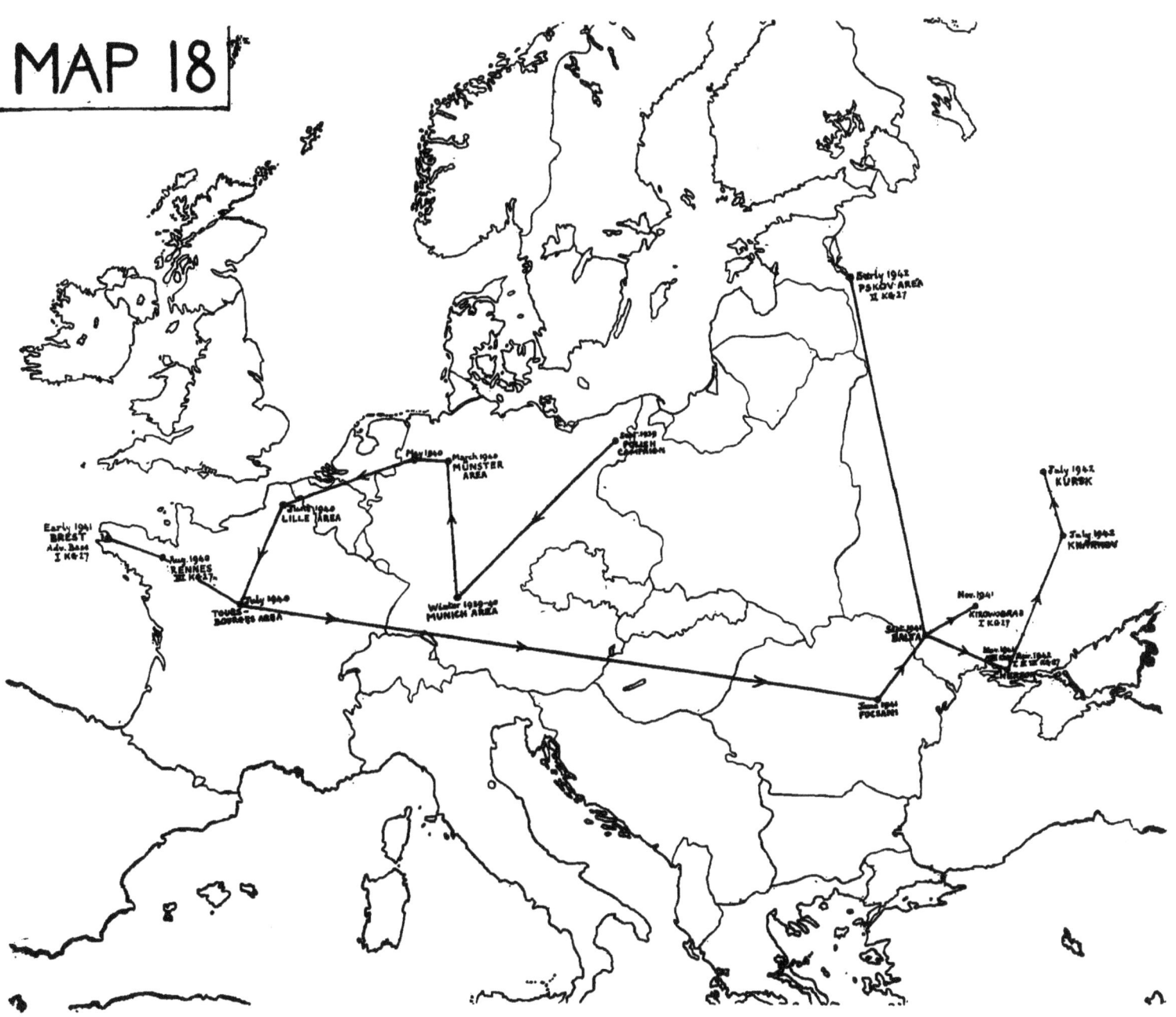

MAP 19

MOVES OF SHORT-RANGE FLYING UNITS ON RUSSIAN FRONT
(June—October, 1941)

The moves of five single-engine fighter and dive-bomber units on the Russian front in the first four months of the offensive against Russia provide useful illustrations of the way such units are handled by the G.A.F.

The offensive opened on 22nd June, 1941. In the North-central zone, the attack, starting from the regions of East Prussia and Brest-Litovsk drove Eastwards in two parallel lines, through Vilna, Lepel and Vitebsk, and through Baranowichi, Minsk and Borisov, in the direction of Smolensk. These drives were checked towards the end of July, after the capture of Smolensk; and the Germans then decided to concentrate their next effort on taking Leningrad. When this effort failed, they turned, at the end of August and in early September, to the completion of the pincer movement closing on the East of Kiev. This pincer was closed towards the end of September; and, next, in early October, the main effort was directed, with feverish intensity, to the capture of Moscow.

Two characteristics in the use of the selected S.E.F. and dive-bomber units stand out during these phases of the offensive. First, the speed with which the flying units were pressed forward, close after each advance of the Army so as to give the Army the maximum support. Secondly, the manner in which the flying units were switched laterally to new sectors to support the attacks to which the High Command gave successive priority. This second characteristic is as much evidence of the inadequacy of the G.A.F. to cover so wide a front as that in Russia as it is of mobility.

Three days after the beginning of the offensive (i.e. 25th June), two dive-bomber Gruppen and three S.E.F. Gruppen moved forward to the line Vilna—Berezovka. Four days later (29th June) they were on the line Widzjuny—Moldechno—Baranowichi, making 130–150 miles advance in the first seven days. By the end of the next seven days (5th July) they had advanced another 130 miles to the line Lepel—Dokudovo. By 21st July they had pressed on still another 100 miles to the line Surash—Demidov—Moscha—Schatalowka (i.e. a little to the West of Smolensk). Each of these moves was close on the heels of the Army. These flying units advanced their bases some 360 miles in a month.

Smolensk fell on 25th July; and, at this stage, as already stated, the main pressure was diverted to the Leningrad front. Two of the five units were transferred there in early August (a move of some 250 miles to the North).

When, at the end of August, it was decided to concentrate all available effort on the Kiev battle, four of the five units (including one which had been on the Leningrad front) were transferred to the Konotop area (i.e. 250 miles South of Smolensk) so as to support the closing of the Northern pincer to the East of Kiev.

Finally, after the conclusion of the Kiev battle, towards the end of September, every available close support unit was based on the Moscow front. Accordingly, in early October, three at least of the units whose moves have been described were transferred to Jucknow to be incorporated in the specially formed Close Support Group which was to assist the Army in its thrust at Moscow from the South-west.

The Units selected for the purpose of this description are II and III Stuka 1, III JG.27, IV JG.51, and III JG.53.

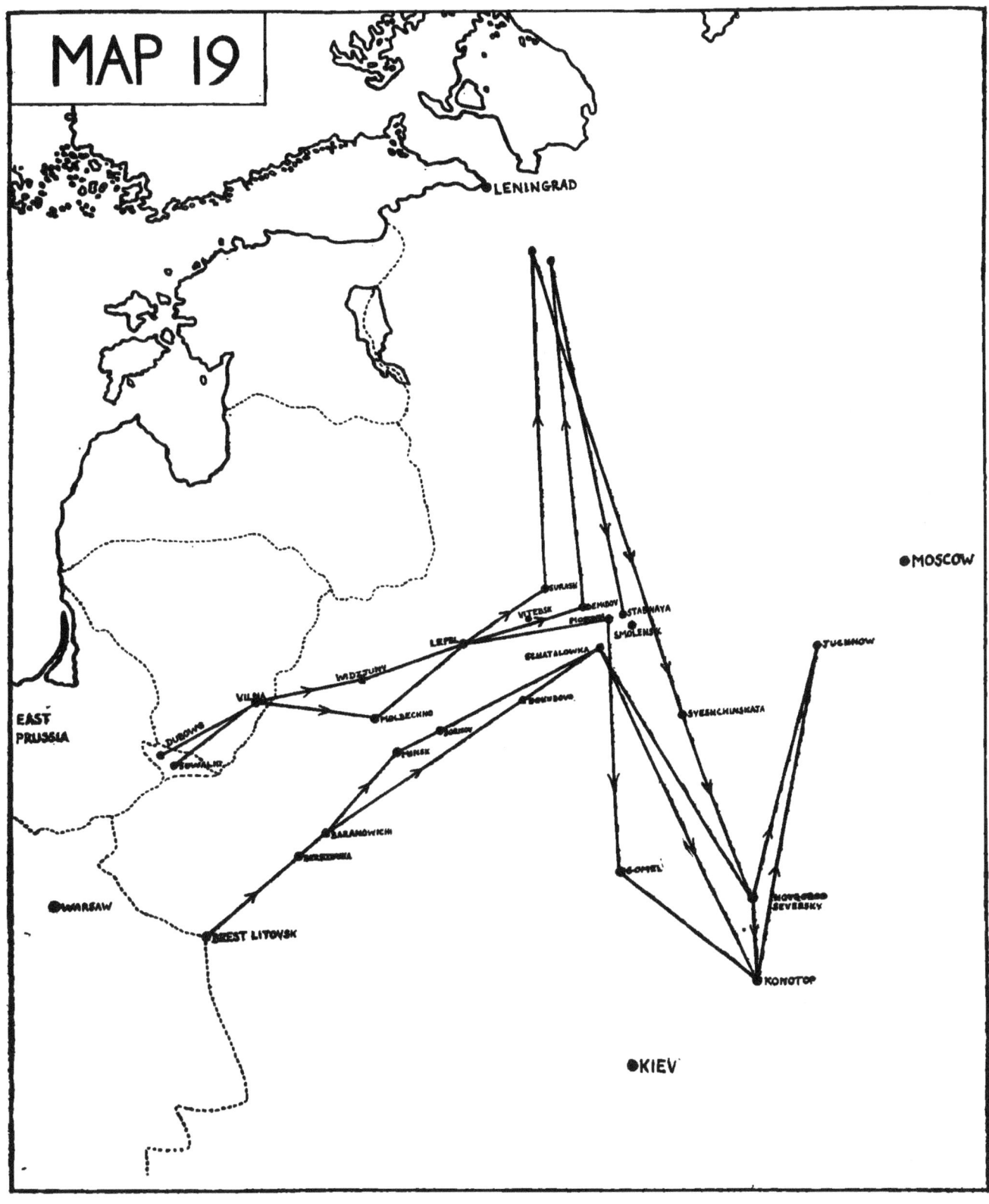

MAP 20

QUICK CONCENTRATION OF FLYING UNITS IN THE BALKANS
(April, 1941)

There were only two occasions prior to 1943 when the Germans had big surprises which impelled them to despatch considerable reinforcements of flying units to danger points at high speed. The first was the unexpected Jugoslav revolution on 27th March, 1941; and the second was the Allied landing in North Africa in November, 1942. (The latter is dealt with in Map 21.)

The Germans had been gradually moving flying units into Rumania (largely round Bucharest) during January, February and early March, 1941. About the middle of March most of these units, consisting of some 400 aircraft, were moved Southward into Bulgaria ready for the attack on Greece. They were based at Sofia, Plovdiv, Krumovo, Krainitzi and Belitza.

It was evident that the Germans did not anticipate that the Yugo-Slavs would do other than co-operate with them in their plans. Suddenly, there was news of the revolution at Belgrade, against the Yugo-Slav Government which had been friendly disposed to Germany. In order to counter this danger to the Germans' right flank, it was necessary for them to attack Belgrade at once.

On 26th March, therefore, orders were given for the rapid transfer of flying units from France, Germany, and the Mediterranean, amounting to nearly 600 aircraft. There were involved :—5 L.R.B. Gruppen (3 from France, 1 from N.W. Germany, and 1 from Sicily); 3 dive-bomber Gruppen (2 from France and 1 from Africa); 6 S.E.F. Gruppen (all from France); 1 T.E.F. Gruppe (from N.W. Germany).

Nearly all the short-range units were to occupy bases at Arad, Deta and Turnu Severin in the extreme West of Rumania, within easy distance of Belgrade. L.R.B. units were to be based on the N.W. and S.E. of Belgrade, at Wiener Neustadt and at Vrba (near Sofia).

The attack on Greece, and on Yugo-Slavia at the same time, started on 6th April; and all, or nearly all, these units had arrived at their destinations with perhaps 75 per cent of their aircraft and were ready to operate (with, say, two-thirds of the 75 per cent) on the opening day.

The method of organising the transfer of units and the dates of arrival naturally varied, but there was a fair amount of uniformity. Usually an advance party and key technical personnel and equipment were sent ahead by transport aircraft. These arrived at their new bases between 1st and 3rd April. The bulk of the operational aircraft arrived between 2nd to 5th April.

The units must have had to borrow M/T for a few days, since this was mostly sent by road owing to congestion on the railways, and did not arrive until about the 9th April at the earliest. Some M/T arrived much later.

It was also, no doubt, possible to borrow ground staff from the G.A.F. personnel already in Rumania and Bulgaria; but G.A.F. flying units have shown that they are able to undertake a fair number of sorties for a week or two with only a small proportion of their normal personnel.

It will be seen that the G.A.F. was on this occasion able to move a fleet of aircraft, comparable in size to a large Fliegerkorps, distances averaging 1,000 miles from bases far apart, so that about 40 to 50 per cent of the establishment number were able to be serviceable for operations in 10 days from the date of the order for transfer. This accomplishment was only possible, first, because the airfields at the destination were ready with assistance in M/T and ground personnel and were capable of being stocked up with fuel, ammunition, etc., from depots within reasonable distance, and, secondly, because a large number of transport aircraft could be made available at short notice.

The two Gruppen moving from North Africa and Sicily respectively naturally had to depend more than the others on assistance at their new temporary bases, though one of them seems to have had about 150–200 men transferred in Ju. 52s.

The lines on the map indicating moves of units are diagrammatic only and do not mark the actual routes followed, which were naturally not straight. The thick line indicates the move of three Gruppen together.

MAP 20

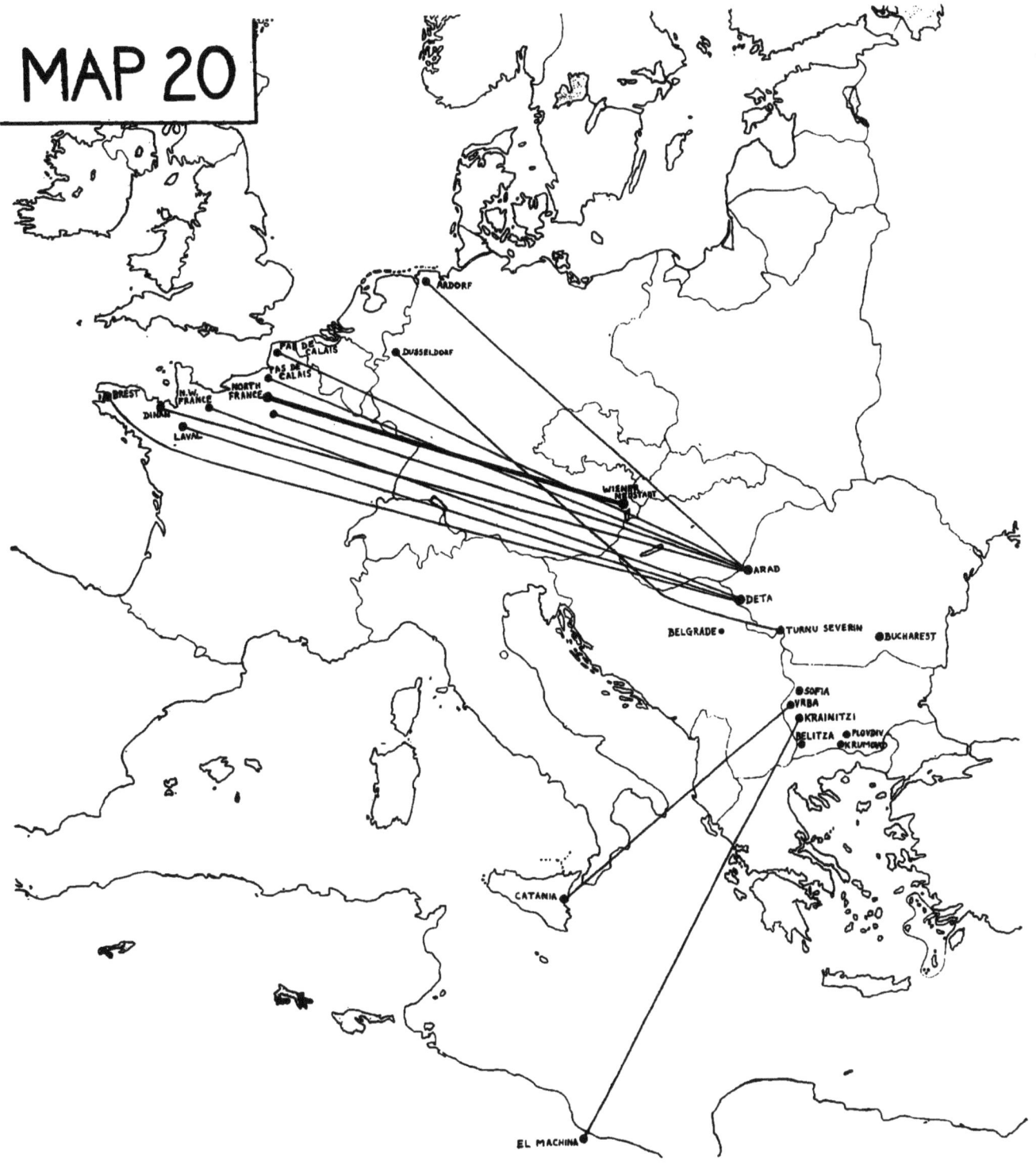

MAP 21

QUICK CONCENTRATION OF FLYING UNITS IN THE MEDITERRANEAN
(November, 1942)

When the Allies made their landings in North Africa on 8th November, 1942, the Germans had their second big surprise of the War. This surprise was different in three respects from that experienced in the Spring of 1941 (see Map 20). In the first place, the Germans were on the defensive; secondly, although airfields in Sicily were ready to accommodate additional units, airfields in Tunisia and in South France were not stocked and staffed ready for operations; and, thirdly, the major commitment of the Russian front had seriously reduced the number of flying units available for transfer. The considerable efforts made by the G.A.F. to concentrate forces at the danger points did not baulk the Allied plans.

There were, at the beginning of November, some 275 aircraft based in Sicily and Sardinia (of which two-thirds were L.R.Bs.); and, in Cyrenaica some 300 aircraft (of which two-thirds were S.E.Fs., including fighter-bombers, etc.).

At the beginning of November it was impossible for the Allies to prevent German reconnaissance suggesting that a considerable Allied sea-borne operation was projected. In the first instance, the Germans apparently concluded that a vast convoy was intended to reinforce the British Eighth Army in Egypt. On or about 2nd November, therefore, four Gruppen of L.R.Bs. (mostly torpedo aircraft) were ordered to move from North Norway to Catania and Comiso in Sicily and to Grosseto in Italy. These Gruppen were thought to have more scope in attacking shipping in the Mediterranean than in operating on the convoy route to Russia. This transfer took from 5 to 9 days, though one staffel claimed to transfer in 48 hours, and other aircraft managed the trip in three days.

Just before the landings, parts of two Gruppen (one of L.R.Bs. and one of T.E.Fs. for escort duties) were transferred from Greece and Crete to Sicily; and when the Germans heard of the landings on 8th November, they ordered parts of another Gruppe of L.R.Bs. from Greece to Sicily and parts of a T.E.F. Gruppe and a long reconnaissance Staffel from Crete to Sicily.

The first moves of flying units to Tunis were rapidly organised. A dive-bomber Gruppe and two S.E.F. Gruppen (which was ferried to Sicily from Sardinia on the previous day) arrived in Tunis on 9th November. This was certainly enterprising since there can have been no more than a handful of improvised ground troops for protection. The first Company of a parachute Regiment did not arrive until the 10th or 11th November, and the ground troops were not even in moderate strength until 13th November.

By 13th November, another S.E.F. Gruppe (which had shortly before been on the Orel front) had reached Bizerta, together with part of a short (Army) reconnaissance Staffel which had been refitting in Weimar (Germany). By 15th November a Gruppe and a further Staffel of S.E.Fs. had moved from Sicily to Bizerta, and a Staffel of long-range reconnaissance aircraft moved from Sicily to Tunis.

For a short time after the landings the Germans evidently apprehended an expedition against the South coast of France or, perhaps, Corsica. Consequently, they moved such units or parts of units as could be spared from Holland, Belgium and North France (including two Reserve Training L.R.B. Gruppen and some S.E.F. training units) to airfields in South France, which region was occupied as soon as the emergency arose.

The Germans had, in previous months, taken some interest in these airfields, but they were not ready for the reception of operational units. For this purpose it required not less than seven days' preparation. About 16th November the following transfers were made:—two L.R.B. Gruppen (partly for mine-laying off Toulon) from Holland to Toulouse and Cognac; one L.R.B. Gruppe from N. France to Istres; two Reserve Training L.R.B. Gruppen from N. France to Toulouse and Montpellier; one T.E.F. Gruppe from Holland and Belgium to Lesignan; one S.E.F. Gruppe from N. France to Marseilles; 20 fighter-bomber aircraft from N. France to Istres; two long reconnaissance Staffeln from N. France to Avignon; two short reconnaissance Staffeln from Germany (lately on the Leningrad front) to Avignon.

Some of the long-range reconnaissance aircraft based at Bordeaux, which normally operated over the Atlantic were diverted for a few days to undertake reconnaissance over the Mediterranean.

The flying units which were moved from North Norway to Sicily and Italy (with nominally 150 aircraft) remained in the Mediterranean after the emergency; but, with the exception of one Gruppe, all the 60 aircraft (being parts of various flying units) which were transferred from Greece and Crete on 7th and 8th November, moved back to their normal bases a few days later.

Nominally 150 (actually, perhaps 125) aircraft were moved to Tunisia, of which over 100 were S.E.Fs. and 25 dive-bombers. Nearly all these remained or were replaced; and additional aircraft were transferred there later.

About 250 aircraft (plus a few from training units) were moved to South France on or about 16th November. Of these some 120 operational aircraft remained; the rest (chiefly L.R.Bs.) returned to their normal bases as soon as the fear of a landing on the South of France was diminished.

Arrangements for the use of transport aircraft were similar to those mentioned in the Note to Map 25. There was, however, one interesting new feature. The dive-bomber Gruppe moving from Sardinia to Tunis used D.F.S. 230 gliders, towed by its own operational aircraft, to carry equipment.

MAP 21

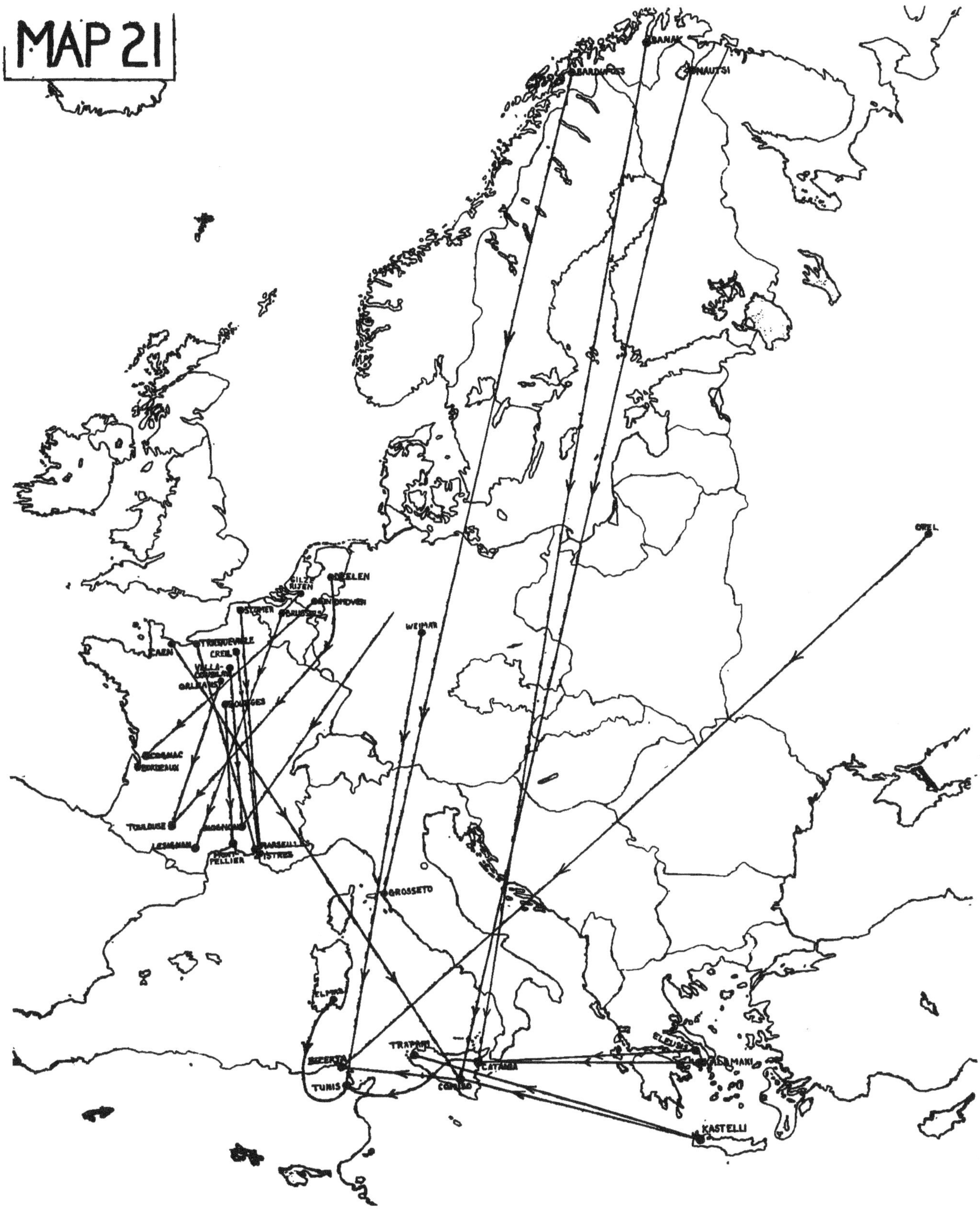
BANAK
OREL
GILZE
RIJEN
CAEN
CREIL
WEIMAR
TOULOUSE
ISTRES
GROSSETO
TRAPANI
CATANIA
TUNIS
ELEUSIS
KASTELLI

DIAGRAM 22

ARMY CO-OPERATION

I.—Air Reconnaissance

1. There are, in the Fliegerkorps, reconnaissance (H) Staffeln, whose task it is to undertake close reconnaissance and artillery spotting for the Army. These Staffeln are organised into Short Reconnaissance Groups. Each Army (or Panzer Army) has, as a normal allocation, one such Group detailed to work with it. On this scale it is usual for each Army Corps (or Panzer Corps) to have one H Staffel allocated to it. Some of the H Staffeln are specially trained and equipped to co-operate with Panzer Corps or Panzer Divisions.

2. The reconnaissance undertaken by an H Staffel includes reporting on troop, tank and artillery positions, field defences in the battle area, and the activity of the opposing Air Force. An H Staffel is highly mobile, and, accordingly, has a liberal establishment of M/T so that it can quickly transfer to a new airfield.

3. There are also long reconnaissance (F) Staffeln working with the Army. These Staffeln are under the command of the Luftflotte (not the Fliegerkorps). They are organised into Long Reconnaissance Groups. The normal allocation is one Group to an Army Group (consisting of several Armies) and one Staffel to an Army (or Panzer Army).

4. The Reconnaissance undertaken by an F Staffel includes reporting on road and railway movements, airfield activity, and defences beyond the battle area.

5. The reports of F Staffeln bear on the larger aspects of tactics; and it is for this reason that these Staffeln are under the Luftflotte, which is in liaison with the higher Army Commands.

6. The subordination of Short and Long Reconnaissance Groups of H and F Staffeln to the Fliegerkorps and Luftflotte, also the allocations to Army Commands are shown in Part II of the Diagram opposite.

7. Prior to 1942, the H and F Staffeln co-operating with the Army were in a separate organisation, outside the Fliegerkorps and Luftflotte, as shown in Part I of the Diagram opposite. They were controlled by officers known as Kolufts who were attached to the Commander in Chief of the Army and to Army Commands. This arrangement proved unsatisfactory, and the new system (Part II of the Diagram) was adopted.

8. In the old system, liaison between the G.A.F. and the Army in regard to reconnaissance was undertaken by the G.A.F. Kolufts. In the new system, this liaison is undertaken by officers called Flivos who are likewise attached to Army Commands for liaison in regard to air support (see para. 14 below). The present liaison between G.A.F. and Army Commands in regard to reconnaissance is shown by dotted lines in Part II of the Diagram.

9. Air to ground communications are made both to the Air Force headquarters and to the Army Command headquarters concerned; also to special ground stations when artillery spotting is done. It is thought that direct communication between reconnaissance aircraft and the leading tanks of armoured formations may have been tested in the field.

II.—Air Support

10. Direct support of the Army by the G.A.F. consists of air attacks on military forces, equipment and stores in the battle area. It frequently happens that Close Support Groups are organised, as *ad hoc* formations, within at Luftflotte for the special purpose of undertaking the direcs support of the Army. These Groups include one to three Stuka, ground-attack, or anti-tank Gruppen (often mixed) and two to four S.E.F. Gruppen.

11. The targets of close-support units are columns of troops, tanks, M/T, artillery and field defence works. These units, however, are sometimes diverted against shipping or to make attacks in the area beyond the battlefield. They sometimes have to undertake their own reconnaissance.

12. Long-range bombers are not infrequently used for direct support of the Army in urgent circumstances. This tendency has been particularly marked on the Russian front. Occasionally a part of a long-range bomber unit has been incorporated in a Close Support group.

13. Indirect support of the Army by the G.A.F. consist of air attacks on:—
   (i) Communications (road, rail and sea) leading to the battle areas.
   (ii) Supply and maintenance depots beyond the battle areas.
   (iii) Airfields from which the Army is being or may be attacked.
   (iv) Aircraft of the opposing Air Force threatening the Army (i.e. attacks on the opposing Air Force in the air).

14. As stated in para. 8 above, in order that co-operation with the Army may be efficiently performed, the Luftflotte and the Fliegerkorps attach air-liaison officers ("Flivos") to appropriate Army Commands. These Flivos pass to the Fliegerkorps headquarters requests by the Army for air support and also tell the Fliegerkorps (for the benefit of its flying units) the positions and intentions of Army formations. Conversely, they supply the Army Commands with particulars of the air support provided and intended to be provided. They have the general obligation of maintaining touch between the two Services in regard to the relations of air and ground tactics.

15. Army formations, which are being given air support communicate with aircraft by means of ground-strips, flags, smoke and light signals and direction shots.

III.—Air Protection

16. The Army expects the G.A.F. to defend it from air attacks. Protection is, therefore, provided in the form of fighter patrols over the battle area. The strength of the patrols depends on the vulnerability of the Army formations concerned (e.g. open flanks) and the weight of the attacks expected. Special measures for fighter protection are required in critical or difficult operations by the Army, for instance armoured spearheads projected rapidly forward, consolidation of bridgeheads, air-landing or embarkation of troops, massing of forces for a fresh attack, or withdrawals, forced and voluntary.

17. S.E.F. units are sometimes detailed for the standing protection of Armies or even Army Corps. Such an allocation may be for any period from a day to some weeks.

18. The type of fighter protection mentioned here must be distinguished from that given to flying units, such as Stukas, ground-attack aircraft and reconnaissance aircraft which are undertaking Army Co-operation.

DIAGRAM 22

PART I
OLD SYSTEM: ARMY RECCE. UNITS ATTACHED TO ARMY.

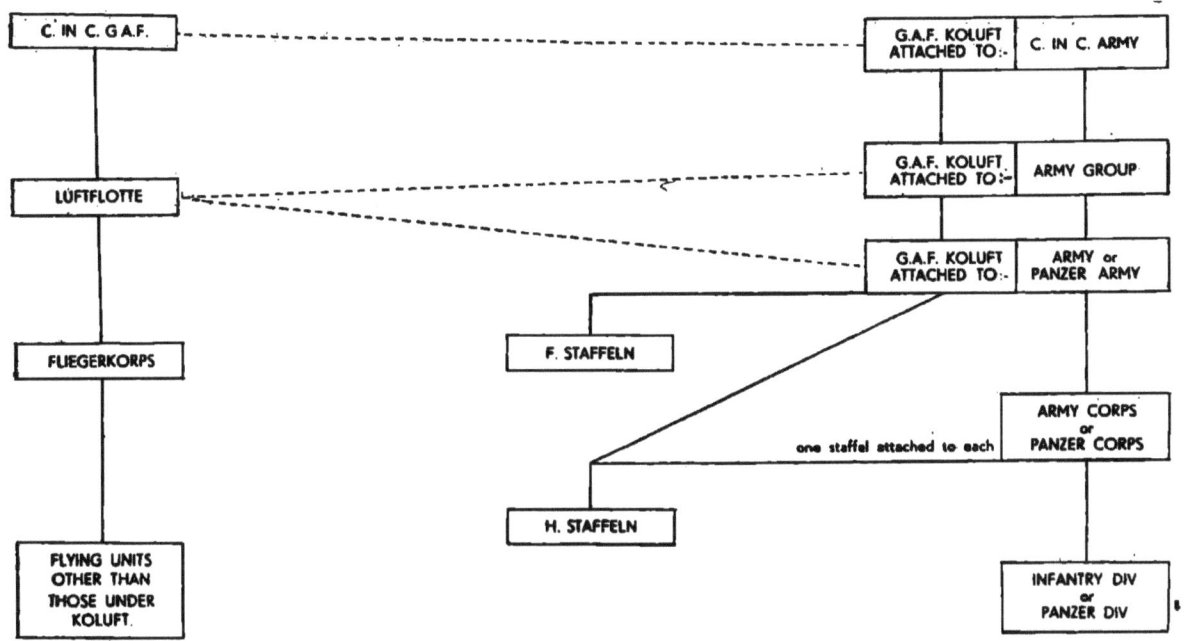

Dotted lines indicate liaison arranged by Kolufts attached to Army Commands.

PART II
NEW SYSTEM: ARMY RECCE. UNITS CONTROLLED BY G.A.F. COMMANDS.

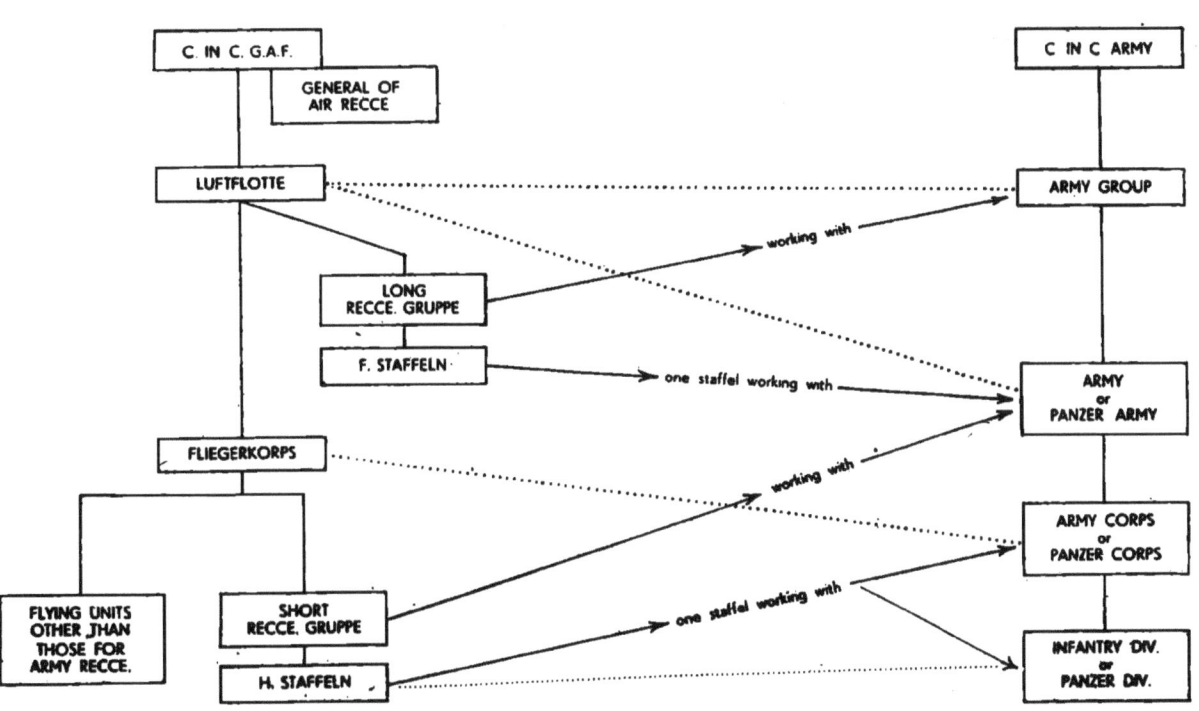

Dotted lines indicate liaison through Flivos attached to Army Commands.

MAP 23

G.A.F. NAVAL CO-OPERATION IN THE WEST, 1942

At the beginning of the war, G.A.F. Naval co-operation in the West was undertaken by a small number of aircraft, chiefly coastal types, operating from N.W. Germany. After the Norwegian campaign and the fall of France, the opportunities for G.A.F. Naval co-operation increased. Commands, such as Fliegerkorps IX, were set up in occupied countries with aircraft operating in the main from Holland; and several O.C. Fighters (Jafues) formed a continuous screen from Norway to France. These Commands were largely occupied in naval co-operation; but naval co-operation by the fighters was naturally additional to their normal defensive operations. Further specialist Commands became necessary as the activities of naval co-operation developed. A Fliegerfuehrer Atlantic was established in West France to take charge of the aircraft based in Brittany and Bordeaux. A Fliegerfuehrer North was put in charge of naval co-operation aircraft based along the West coast (and later North East) of Norway.

After the opening of the Russian campaign, in the summer of 1941, the need was found for another new Fliegerfuehrer whose command was concerned with aircraft operating in the N.E. of Norway; and, when the G.A.F. was called on to intensify its attacks on British convoys to Russia, still another Fliegerfuehrer (with aircraft based near the Lofoten Islands) was established in order to supersede a previous organisation of flying units in that area. As a result, Fliegerfuehrer North became divided into Fliegerfuehrer North (West) and Fliegerfuehrer North (East), with the new Fliegerfuehrer Lofoten operating between them.

Commands under Fliegerfuehrers consist of flying units composed of mixed types of aircraft which cannot conveniently come directly under the charge of a Fliegerkorps or Luftflotte owing to the special nature of their tasks and to geographical considerations.

A brief classification of the types of activity included in naval co-operation is given in Appendix F.

Some particulars of the various Commands concerned with naval co-operation in the West, the areas covered by them, their bases and the nature of their activities for the period January 1942 to January 1943 are given in tabular form below.

COMMANDS	AREAS COVERED	BASES	ACTIVITIES
FLIEGERKORPS IX (1) Bomber and minelaying units (2) Long reconnaissance units	Whole coastal area of British Isles, including West coasts. Southernmost part of North Sea, especially East Anglian coast from Yorkshire to Kent inclusive. Western end of English Channel and S.W. approaches to British Isles.	In Holland In Holland In Brittany	Attacks on shipping in harbours and at sea; minelaying. Reconnaissance. Reconnaissance.
O.C. FIGHTERS, NORWAY	West and S.W. coastal areas of Norway	Stavanger, Trondheim, Bergen, Oslo, also Bardufoss.	Close reconnaissance and close escort; occasional offensives.
O.C. FIGHTERS, HELIGOLAND BIGHT	Heligoland Bight	In Denmark and N.W. Germany	Close reconnaissance and close escort; occasional offensives.
O.C. FIGHTERS, HOLLAND	Off West coast of Holland extending to sea area off East Anglian coast.	In Holland	Close reconnaissance, harbour reconnaissance, close escort; occasional offensives.
O.C. FIGHTERS 2	Straits of Dover and harbours at S.E. coast of England	In Belgium and Pas de Calais..	Close reconnaissance, harbour reconnaissance, close escort; occasional offensives.
O.C. FIGHTERS 3	English Channel and S.W. coast harbours	In N.W. France	Close reconnaissance, harbour reconnaissance, close escort; occasional offensives.
FLIEGERFUEHRER ATLANTIC	East Atlantic, including Bay of Biscay, North coast of Spain, coast of Portugal; approaches to Gibraltar and Gulf of Cadiz; St. George's Channel; West of Ireland and special course round N.W. of Ireland to Stavanger. Reconnaissance area extends Westward to about 20 deg. W.	In Brittany Peninsula; Bordeaux chiefly for long reconnaissances.	Reconnaissance, including meteorological, defensive and armed reconnaissance; offensives; air escort; anti-submarine patrols.
FLIEGERFUEHRER NORTH (WEST)..	North Sea, including Skagerrak, Kattegat and Heligoland Bight, harbours on East of Scotland and Northwards; area between West Norway, North Scotland and Iceland; to S.W. and North of Iceland including Iceland harbours; occasionally as far as Denmark Strait and Greenland, occasionally N.W. and even West of Scotland. As far North as 70 deg. N. (or rarely to 75 deg. N.) and about 15 deg. E.	Bergen, Trondheim, Stavanger, Aalborg.	As preceding, also ice reconnaissance and photo reconnaissance of harbours and anchorages.
FLIEGERFUEHRER NORTH (EAST)	North of Norway and Eastwards along coast to White Sea and occasionally to Nova Zembla; Kola Peninsula, Murmansk, Archangel; area between North Cape and Bear Island; occasionally to Spitzbergen. Westward to about 20 deg. E.	Banak, Kirkenes	Reconnaissance, including meteorological, ice, defensive, and armed reconnaissance; air escort; anti-submarine patrols; occasional offensives including fighter-bomber and Stuka operations against shipping in Kola Inlet and Murmansk.
FLIEGERFUEHRER LOFOTEN	Sea area West, N.W. and North of Lofoten, extending Westwards a little North of Iceland; Northwards to about 78 deg. N.; Eastwards to about 25 deg. E.; Southward to about 67 deg. N.; occasionally down to Trondheim to land.	Bardufoss, Tromsoe, Sorreisa, Bodoe.	Reconnaissance, including meteorological, ice, defensive and armed reconnaissance; air escort; anti-submarine patrols; occasional offensives.

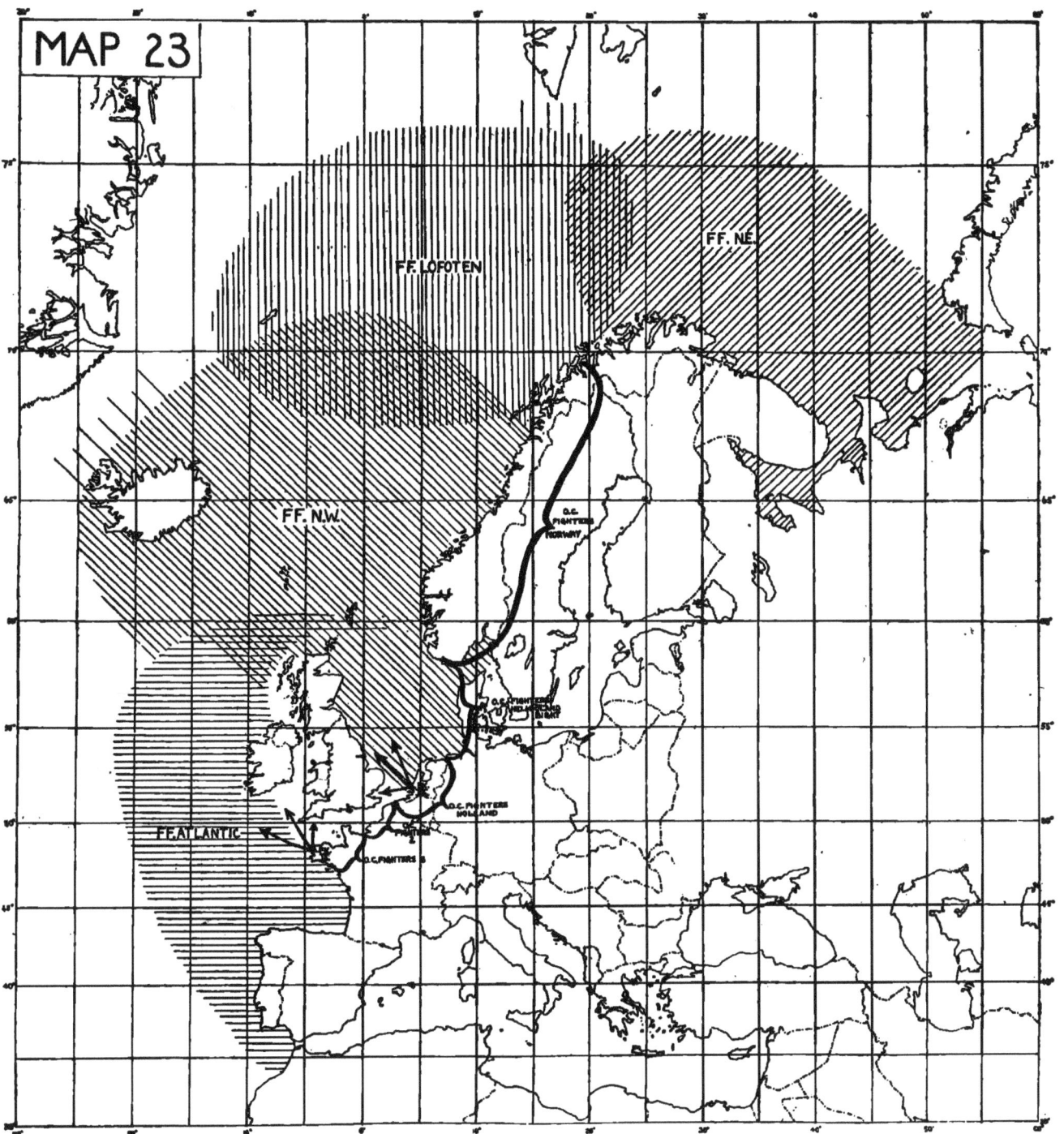

MAP 24

AIR TRANSPORT IN THE MEDITERRANEAN
Rommel in Egypt (July—November, 1942)

On a battle-front such as that in Russia, transport aircraft of the G.A.F. are chiefly used to reinforce or replace M/T as a means of transport in the area between the railheads and the forward airfields. Their use is, of course, specially valuable where road communications are bad or speed is important.

During the campaign in North Africa the primary means of transport was by sea. When, as often happened, sea transport could not be relied upon, air transport was not merely a useful accessory, but an essential one. In fact, the Germans could not have carried on the campaign without it. The period between June, 1942 and January, 1943 is, therefore, chosen to portray in two maps the changes in the air transport routes which were necessitated as the battle moved from Egypt to Tunisia. The course of events in this period well illustrate both the potentialities and the limitations of air transport in the G.A.F. (For some general remarks on G.A.F. Air Transport, see Diagram 26 and Appendix G.)

The same period also illustrates the alternative preference for transport of personnel (chiefly for the Army), on the one hand, and for transport of supplies, on the other. At some stages the Germans were impelled to use air transport of personnel not only for speed but also owing to the high risk of their loss at sea. Personnel could not be replaced, whereas goods could be. But, from time to time, acute shortage of supplies, especially fuel, caused by sinkings, forced the Germans to give preference to transport of supplies at the expense of personnel.

Owing to the difficulties of railway communications through the Balkans, only a limited transport of personnel and supplies was possible by that route. The main route of supplies to the German forces in North Africa was *via* Italy. This fact, together with the limitation in range of the Ju. 52 aircraft to 500 miles and the need for avoiding refuelling in North Africa led to the adoption, first, of the route Italy—Greece—Crete—Cyrenaica; next, Italy—Sicily—Tripoli; and, finally, Italy—Sicily—Tunisia.

The map opposite covers the period from the end of June, 1942 (when Rommel reached El Alamein) to 2nd November, 1942 (when the British Eighth Army broke through Rommel's defences). During this period the large majority of personnel and supplies was transported by the routes marked in heavy lines. The flights were broken in Crete so as to save refuelling at Tobruk. The number of transport aircraft available at this stage was about 200–250. There were probably 50 to 60 per cent of them serviceable on the average, but not all of these would have been used except in the more urgent situations.

It is estimated that, in the three months of July, August and September, about 46,000 men (in 2,600 "lifts" of 18 men per aircraft) and 3,800 tons of supplies (in 1,900 "lifts" of 2 tons per aircraft) were transported to Africa. The maximum number of personnel carried in a single day was 1,000; and an average of 750 men per day was maintained over a considerable period.

Shortage of fuel for operational aircraft and for M/T must have caused frequent anxiety; but the most acute shortage of fuel was in October owing to heavy losses at sea. The Panzer Army was specially in need. The whole of the available transport aircraft, as well as some operational types such as He. 111s, were employed in transport of fuel. It seems probable that the amount delivered by air to the Panzer Army during October was at least as great as, and may well have exceeded, the quantity received from the ships which escaped destruction.

During the period covered by this map, the administration of the air transport fleet in the Mediterranean was under the direction of an O.C. Air Transport at Rome, who had subordinate offices in Brindisi, Athens, Crete and Africa.

The main routes are marked in the Map opposite with heavy lines.

MAP 24

MAP 25

AIR TRANSPORT IN THE MEDITERRANEAN
Rommel's Defeat and the Opening of the Tunisian Campaign (November, 1942 to January, 1943)

When, in early November, 1942, Rommel was driven out of Egypt, air transport was specially valuable to him in his retreat, for often he did not know what port he could rely on for sea transport.

The G.A.F. Air Transport in the Mediterranean had, at the same period, another exacting task to undertake. It had to play a leading part in the rapid establishment and consolidation of the Axis bridgehead in Tunisia as a counter-move to the Allied landings from 8th November onwards.

The number of transport aircraft made available for these tasks was about 350-400 in November and December, 1942. But this number fell to about 250 when the Eastern air-route could no longer be used.

Tobruk, which had been the main African terminus in the preceding months, was abandoned by the Germans on 11th November. During the ensuing week, as Rommel was retreating Westwards, temporary termini were improvised at airfields in Cyrenaica (as shown in the map opposite), until the limit of range of Ju. 52s from Crete was reached, namely at Magrum.

During the time that Rommel was in the El Agheila area a little to the East of Arco (in the latter part of November and early December), it was impossible for supplies to reach him by Ju. 52s, and there was no adequate seaport nearby. He had, therefore, to rely on such supplies as could be transported from Tripoli and even from Tunisia, together with those transported from the heel of Italy in long-range aircraft such as He. 111s and a few F.W. 200s.

At the same period, reinforcements and supplies, which had been collected in Greece for transport by the Eastern air-route and were now wanted in Tunisia, had to be flown from Athens to South Italy and Sicily to be carried to North Africa by the Western air-route.

There was a considerable traffic on the route Italy—Sicily—Tripoli from mid-November until Tripoli was captured by the Allies on 23rd January.

The air transport organisation, in supplying the Axis bridgehead in Tunisia, used the route Italy—Sicily—Tunisia. Not only were Ju. 52s employed, but also large powered gliders, Me. 323s which carry 10 tons, this being the first occasion of their inclusion in the air transport fleet.

We have learnt from captured documents that, during December, 1942 and January, 1943, over 19,000 men of the German Army and Air Force and 4,500 tons of supplies and equipment were carried by air to Tunis alone. Of these amounts, 18,000 men and 3,000 tons were taken by Ju. 52. The corresponding figures for Me. 323 were 1,250 men and 1,475 tons. The average daily effort in aircraft was 50 "lifts" (i.e. 90 tons) by Ju. 52 and 3 "lifts" (or 30 tons) by Me. 323.

From the middle of November onwards, the administration of the air transport fleet was no longer under the sole command of the O.C. Air Transport, Rome. The command was divided in two, there being an O.C. Air Transport at Rome and another at Athens, each having such subordinate offices as might be necessary.

The main routes are marked in the Map opposite with heavy lines.

This Map may be usefully compared with Map 17.

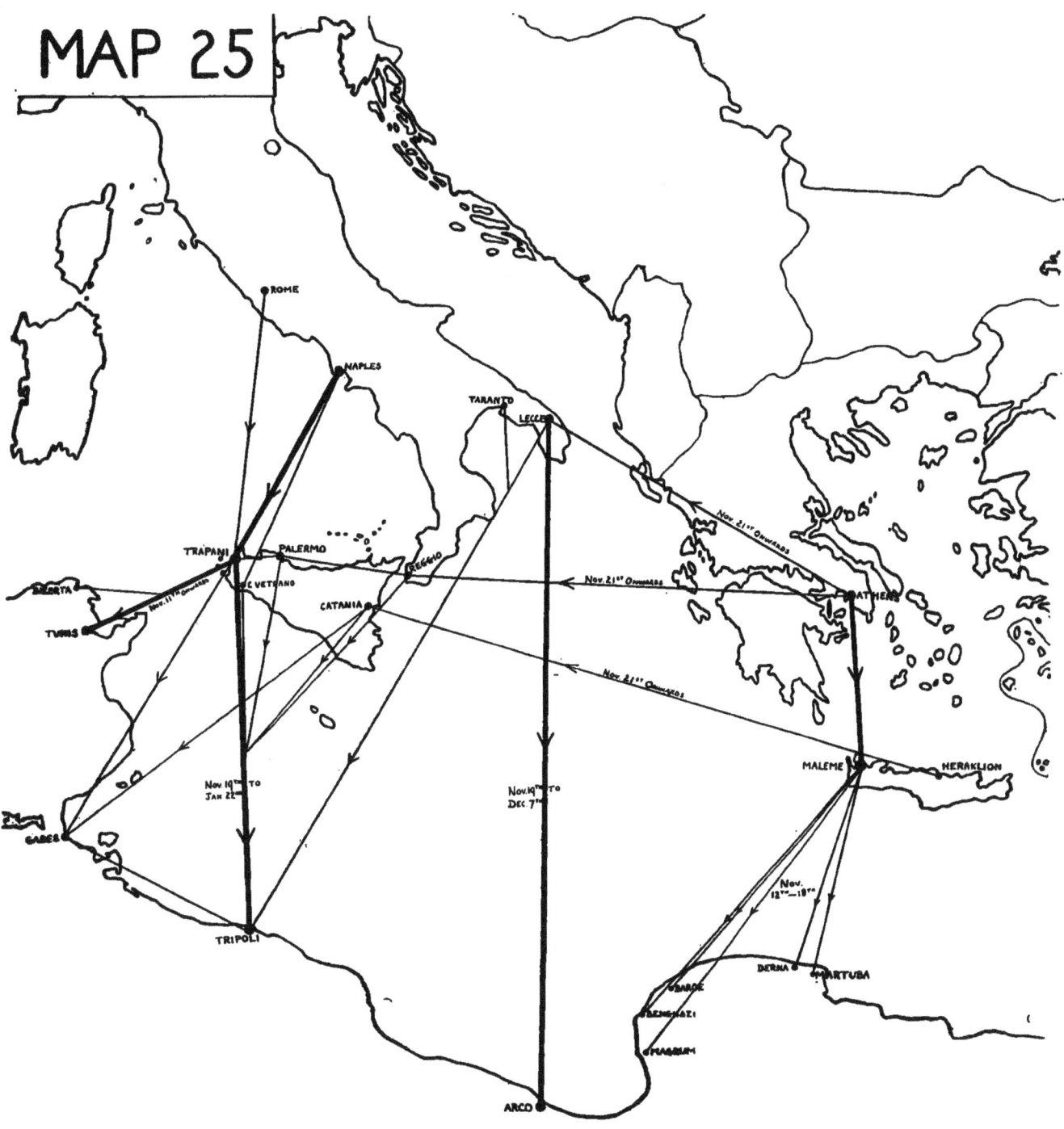

DIAGRAM 26

ORGANISATION OF AIR TRANSPORT

1. Composition of Units

In 1942 there were about 2,300 transport-type aircraft of all kinds in the G.A.F., of which about 1,200 were Ju. 52s, 200 He. 111s, 50 Me. 323s, and 450 miscellaneous types for lighter work. In addition there were about 300 tugs for gliders, and about 500 gliders for carrying freight or troops.

Of the 1,200 Ju. 52s., some 400 to 500 are regularly used in flying training schools. In the past, some of these aircraft have been called out for transport work when such crises arose as the encirclement of a German Army at Stalingrad; but the resultant disorganisation of bomber training makes it unlikely that this practice will continue.

The 300 glider tugs are organised into five Gruppen of 48 aircraft each, and are normally reserved for the training and operations of parachute and airborne troops under Fliegerkorps XI.

This leaves some 1,000 heavy aircraft for regular transport duties. The basic unit is the Gruppe of 53 aircraft, composed of four Staffeln (12 aircraft each) and a Gruppe Staff with five aircraft. About 20 of these Gruppen are formed into Geschwader of four Gruppen each. Further Gruppen may be formed temporarily according to need. There are also other small formations of transport aircraft attached to Commands (see below).

The personnel of a Gruppe (both flying and ground staff) number 350 to 400. An Airfield Servicing Company of 180 men is in addition allocated to each Gruppe.

2. General Control

Air Transport is regarded as part of the supply organisation of the G.A.F. The supreme control of the transport Gruppen is therefore vested in Dept. 4 of the General Staff at the Air Ministry, which Department also arranges the strategic allocation of supplies to the various fronts. (See Diagram opposite.)

When transport Gruppen are allocated to a front, the General Staff delegates operational control of them to the Luftflotte Commander in whose area they are to work. He exercises this control through his Chief Quartermaster. All requests for air transport space by lower G.A.F. Commands or units in the Luftflotte area must be addressed to the Luftflotte Chief Quartermaster, unless (as sometimes happens) he has detailed one or more Gruppen to work under the orders of a Luftgau or Fliegerkorps Command for the duration of a specific task. It must be emphasised that there is no standard allocation of Transport Gruppen to a Luftflotte. This depends entirely on needs, and may range from one to sixteen Gruppen. The Luftflotte Commander must apply to Dept. 4 of the General Staff if he requires an increase of transport Gruppen in his area.

The transport Gruppen are often employed on moving troops, equipment or supplies for the Army. When operations of limited scope are involved, the Army Commander in the area can obtain air transport space by applying to the Luftflotte Commander; but if operations are of a major character, the request is put through at War Ministry and Air Ministry level. When the interests of the G.A.F. and the Army conflict, the C.-in-C. Armed Forces doubtless settles which is to have prior claim. But, given the task, the tactical execution remains under G.A.F. control, and no Army Command is permitted to issue direct orders for the employment of Air Transport units.

Besides the transport Gruppen, there are many smaller air transport formations. Each Fliegerkorps has permanently allocated to it a Transport Staffel of 12 to 18 heavy aircraft, which it uses without reference to the Luftflotte for carrying supplies and equipment to its subordinate flying units. (The Fliegerkorps would naturally apply to the Luftflotte Chief Quartermaster for the loan of further transport aircraft when a considerable movement of flying units was due to take place). Also within Fliegerkorps control are the Courier Staffeln, each usually with 12 aircraft of assorted types, that operate between the Air Reconnaissance Groups and Army H.Q. near the battle fronts; and the Liaison Staffeln, each of about 12 small aircraft capable of landing on improvised strips near the front line, which maintain liaison between G.A.F. Close Support formations and the Battle H.Q. of Army formations. (See Diagram.)

The Luftgau or Special Luftgau Staff has no regular establishment of transport aircraft, but at the discretion of the Luftflotte Chief Quartermaster may be allowed to control the operations of up to two transport Gruppen for a determinable period. Luftgaus are also sometimes ordered by the Luftflotten to set up and maintain a Courier Staffel for transporting officers, mails, and despatches within stated limits. But such minor units, like the Courier Staffeln attached to the Service Ministries in Germany, and the "Duty Flights" which may be attached to a Luftflotte H.Q., play a very small part in the main G.A.F. transport organisation.

So far, only the operational control of air transport units has been considered. There remains the question of internal administration of personnel engaged in the air transport services; and that of apportioning aircraft among the transport Gruppen and maintaining their serviceability. This administrative control, like the operational control, rests finally in the hands of Dept. 4 of the General Staff at the Air Ministry. But subordinate to that Department in Germany there is a staff, once known as O.C. Air Transport, Berlin, and now thought to be a Fliegerkorps, to which the management of all questions touching air transport personnel and aircraft is delegated. This Fliegerkorps has regional Transport Fliegerfuhrers in areas where numerous transport Gruppen are operating, and is responsible for maintaining supplies of crews and aircraft. It supervises the training of air transport crews and the repair of transport aircraft at German airfields or factories.

Some remarks on the kinds of employment of air transport and types of aircraft and freight are given in Appendix G.

DIAGRAM 26

ORGANISATION OF AIR TRANSPORT

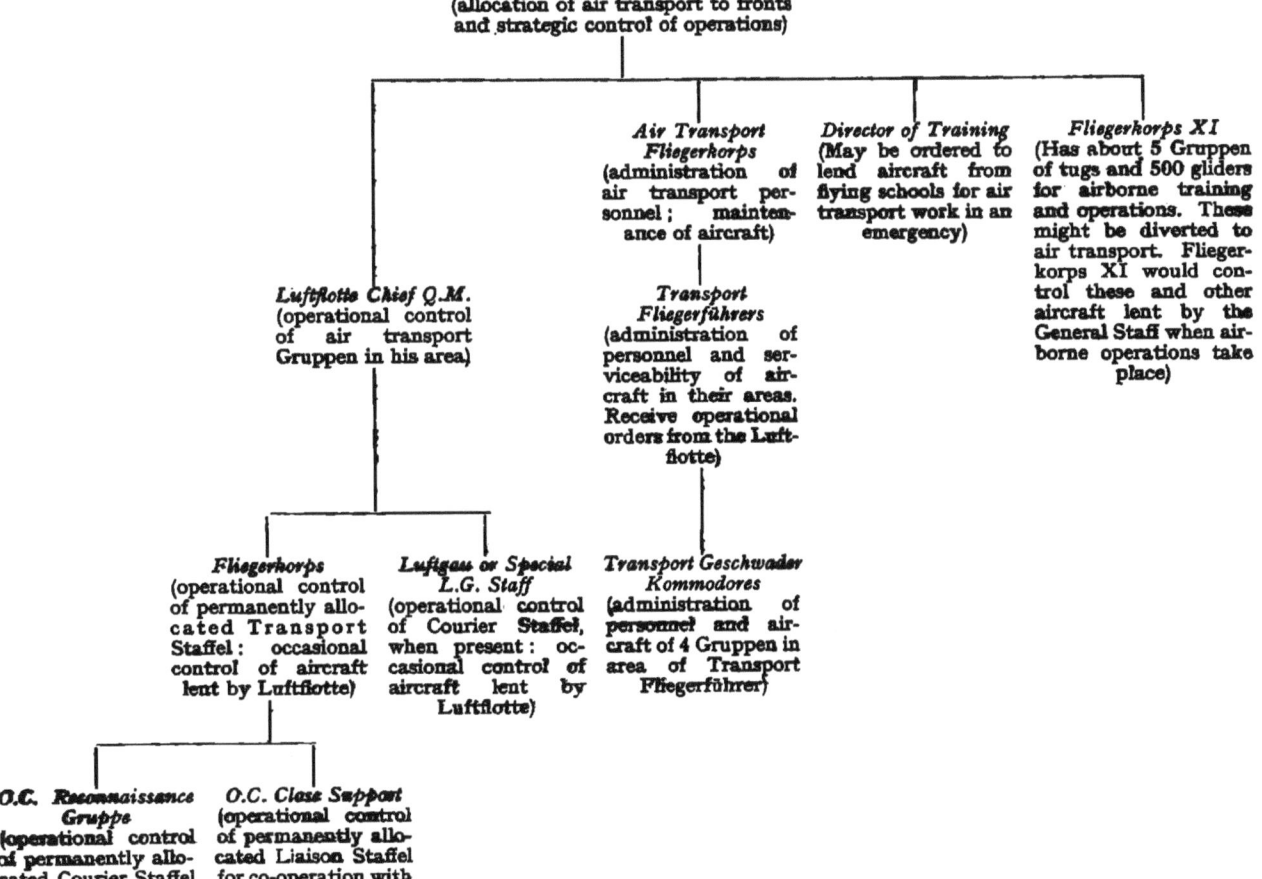

DIAGRAM 27

PROVISION AND MAINTENANCE OF AIRCRAFT

Part I — Provision of Aircraft

The German Air Ministry's stocks of new aircraft are, after delivery from the factories, stored and prepared for issue at Air Ministry Equipment Depots in Germany, of which there are seven of this kind (see Map 29). Alternatively new aircraft may be stored at specified Parks in Germany.

The Air Ministry, through its General Staff (Department 6) and its Director General of Equipment, maintains a close control over the provision of new aircraft. The scales of issue are determined by the General Staff, but the actual provision of aircraft is arranged by the Director General of Equipment.

The allotment of aircraft by the Air Ministry may be to the Luftflotte, to be held in the Luftflotte reserve of aircraft, and re-allotted to flying units as required. Alternatively, in such instances as considerable replacements, the allotment by the Air Ministry may be direct to flying units with due notice to the Luftflotte, which in turn would inform the Fliegerkorps. The Equipment Groups in each Luftgau are not so closely concerned in the issue of aircraft as they are with that of equipment and supplies, but they assist in and keep records of allotments of aircraft.

Delivery of new aircraft is made from the Equipment Depot (or Park) to Commands or flying units.

Luftflotte reserves of aircraft may, if circumstances allow, be held at Parks in Germany. But the deployment of Luftflotten on battle-fronts has necessitated the establishment of Aircraft Distributing Centres and Aircraft Forwarding Stations in occupied countries. When desirable, the components of new aircraft are sent in crates to these Stations by rail and are assembled there. A Luftflotte may have several Aircraft Forwarding Stations, one for each main type of aircraft.

Ferrying of new aircraft from the Depots in Germany to the distributing stations in the Luftflotte areas in occupied countries is undertaken by special ferrying units controlled by the Director General of Equipment and Equipment Groups.

When flying units are ordered by the Air Ministry to be re-equipped with new types of aircraft, one or more suitably situated and equipped G.A.F. Stations is selected for the purpose. Gruppen engaged in operations on battle-fronts are sometimes re-equipped with new aircraft a Staffel at a time.

Part I of the diagram on the opposite page shows the possible channels of delivery. The chain of control is spaced to correspond with the channels of delivery.

Part II — Maintenance of Aircraft

Simple repairs to aircraft are undertaken by the workshop platoons of Airfield Servicing Companies attached to flying units. But the maintenance system proper may be said to start at the bottom with the repair hangar (Werft) on the airfield, which is staffed by the Airfield Command, under the Luftgau. All repairs within their scope are effected in these repair hangars.

The arrangements for maintenance of aircraft in Germany naturally differ considerably from those in occupied countries and on battle-fronts. In Germany, all the more important airfields have well-equipped repair hangars; but on battle-fronts, there may be no repair hangar or only an inadequate improvisation.

In order to save as far as possible the sending of aircraft back to Germany from battle-fronts for repairs, an organisation of Field Workshop Units (composed of Platoons with mobile workshops and plant) was established. These are stationed at many airfields on battle-fronts, especially where there is a paucity of repair facilities.

When, in occupied countries, there has been time to utilize the machinery of aircraft factories for aircraft repair, these factories are requisitioned and staffed with personnel from factories in Germany assisted by local labour. They are called Front Repair Works, and are generally capable of undertaking heavy repairs. This expedient has been used in France, Holland, Belgium, Norway, Greece, Poland, and South Russia.

Another method of dealing with heavy repairs is to order them to be carried out at specified G.A.F. Stations in Germany or well back from the line. The directions in each instance are given by the Equipment Group of the Luftgau which is the office concerned with equipment and supplies. Occasionally flying units operating on battle-fronts are allotted auxiliary bases (situated closer to them than their home bases in Germany). These bases are used for heavy repairs as occasion may arise.

In the most difficult kinds of repair the Equipment Group in the Luftgau may have to arrange for aircraft to be sent to one of the factories in Germany which manufacture the type of aircraft concerned. Such repairs are watched by the Air Ministry's factory inspectors.

General control over the maintenance of aircraft from the operational point of view is exercised by the General Staff (Department 6) at the Air Ministry. General technical control is undertaken by the Director General of Equipment at the Air Ministry.

Repairs to aircraft in the repair hangars on airfields are under the administration of the Luftgau authorities; and, as remarked above, the Equipment Group of the Luftgau has special responsibilities in this respect.

The Director General of Equipment has particular charge of the Field Workshop Units and the Front Repair Works, which he evidently organised as special war-time expedients to improve the serviceability of operational aircraft on battle-fronts by providing maintenance facilities close to the operational airfields.

The various alternative means of maintenance of aircraft are set out in tabular form in Part II of the diagram on the opposite page, together with tabulated particulars regarding the controlling authorities.

DIAGRAM 27

PROVISION AND MAINTENANCE OF AIRCRAFT

PART I — Provision of Aircraft

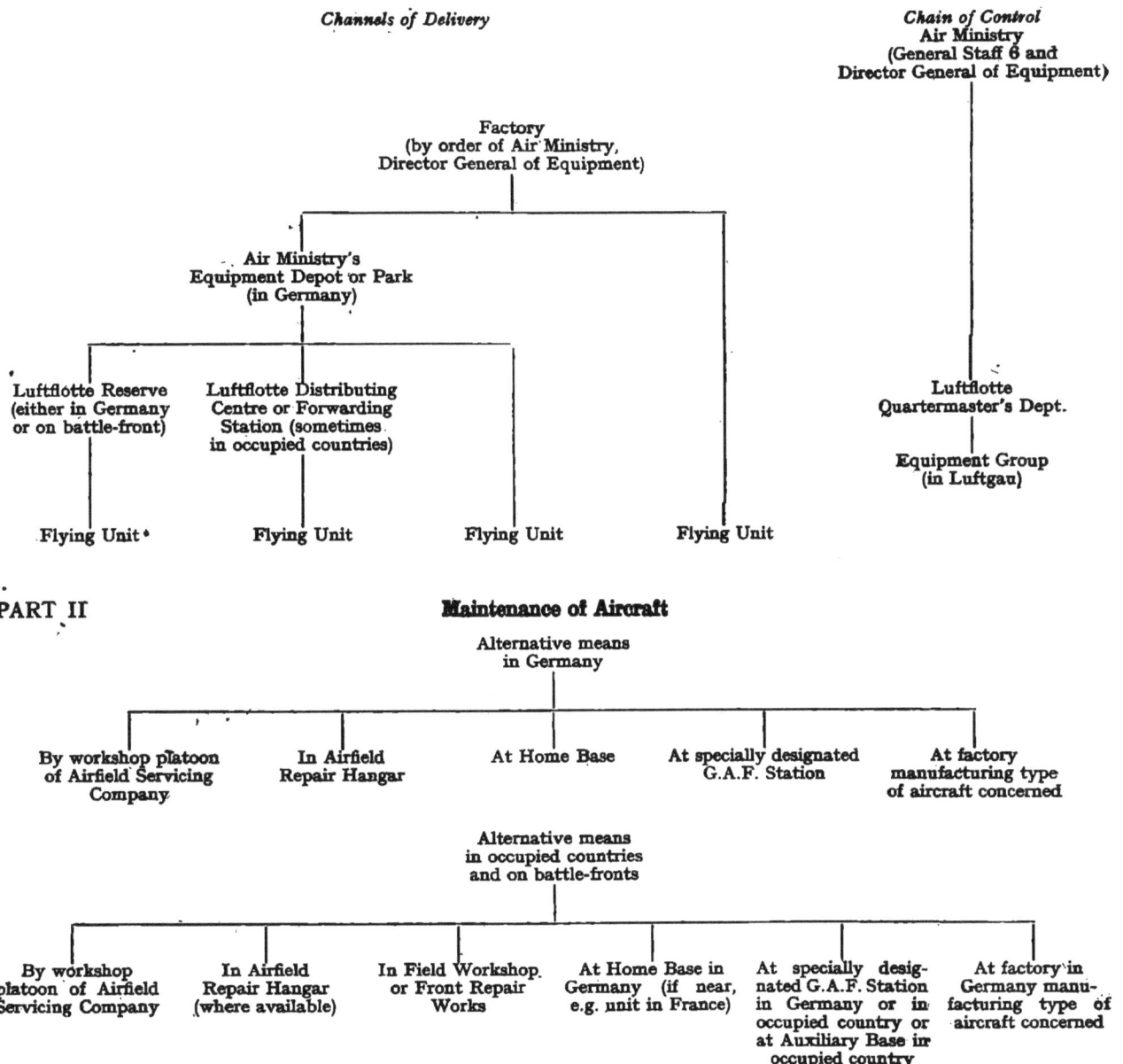

Control of maintenance arrangements:—
- General control from operational point of view :—General Staff (Dept. 6).
- General control from technical point of view :—Director General of Equipment.
- In repair hangars on airfields :—Equipment Group of Luftgau and Luftgau personnel lower in scale.
- Field Workshops :—Special charge of Director General of Equipment, but operationally under Luftflotten, and may be attached to Fliegerkorps and/or to Luftgaus as required.
- Front Repair Works :—Special charge of Director General of Equipment, who is in touch with the factories in Germany which provide the staffs.

DIAGRAM 28

PROVISION OF SUPPLIES AND AIRCRAFT EQUIPMENT

Part I *Provision of Supplies*

Supplies are distinguishable from equipment in that they are consumed in the course of being used, e.g. fuel, ammunition, rations.

The General Staff at the Air Ministry (Department 4) decides, from the operational point of view, what supplies are to be issued. The Director General of Equipment at the Air Ministry is responsible for the issue of supplies (as well as equipment).

The supplies manufactured to the order of the Director General of Equipment are first stored in Main Fuel Depots and Main Ammunition Depots in Germany, whence they are allocated on proper authority to Luftgaus in Germany or " forward " Luftgaus in occupied countries. The office in the Luftgau responsible for the issue of supplies in that area is the Equipment Group.

In Germany, aircraft fuel and ammunition are generally delivered from the Main Depots direct by rail to the airfields, though some miscellaneous supplies are delivered through the Air Park of the Equipment Group.

Most of the storage of fuel and ammunition in Luftgau areas in occupied countries is in Field Tank Depots and Field Ammunition Depots, whence the supplies may be transported either direct to airfields or *via* forward dumps.

Forward dumps may be in the open with improvised protection. Fuel in dumps may be in barrels or in trucks.

Field depots and forward dumps are operated by specially trained bodies of men in Supply Companies. Sometimes there are Ammunition Issuing Stations or Fuel Issuing Stations.

Transport of supplies is by rail, canal or river where practicable; and these means will generally be adopted in Germany. Alternatively, supplies may be delivered by M/T Supply Columns (either Transport Columns or Fuel Columns). In urgent circumstances or in stages of a campaign when the transport system has not had time to be developed, they may be delivered by air.

Part I of the diagram on the opposite page shows the possible channels of delivery. Supplies to units in Germany may go by routes 1 or 2; and those for units in the field may go by routes 3, 4 or 5.

The chain of control is spaced to correspond with the channels of delivery. The Field Depots and Field Air Parks are shown to be under the charge of the Equipment Group of the Luftgau; and the forward dumps are controlled by the Supply Stations attached to the Airfield Regional Commands.

Part II *Provision of Aircraft Equipment*

The main stocks of aircraft equipment are stored at the Air Ministry Equipment Depots in Germany, some of which specialise in particular kinds of aircraft engines or equipment (see Map 29). The office in each Luftgau called the Equipment Group controls the issue of equipment within the Luftgau. The main Luftgau stocks of equipment are stored in one or more Air Parks or (in occupied countries or on battle-fronts) in Field Air Parks.

A further decentralisation is necessary on battle-fronts, where there are Equipment Issuing Stations at or near the main airfields of Airfield Regional Commands, or smaller and more mobile ones at or near the airfields occupied by short-range units. These smaller Equipment Issuing Stations, dealing in equipment for particular types of aircraft, are fully motorised, and are even occasionally carried by air. Sometimes Equipment Issuing Stations are housed in several railway trucks; but these will generally be for long-range aircraft.

The Field Workshop units which undertake maintenance of aircraft on battle-fronts hold small stocks of spare equipment or have Equipment Issuing Stations close at hand.

Equipment urgently required and not in stock in Equipment Issuing Stations is delivered by air from Air Parks or even Equipment Depots; and air transport may be extensively used for delivery of aircraft equipment where the transport system is inadequate.

Part II of the diagram on the opposite page shows the possible channels of delivery. Aircraft equipment for units in Germany may go by routes 1 or 2; and that for units in the field may go by routes 3, 4 or 5; 1 and 3 are the normal routes.

The chain of control is spaced to correspond with the channels of delivery. The Air Parks or Field Air Parks are shown to be under the charge of the Equipment Group of the Luftgau; and the Equipment Issuing Stations in occupied countries or on battle-fronts have the double function of storage of equipment and control of its issue.

DIAGRAM 28

PROVISION OF SUPPLIES AND AIRCRAFT EQUIPMENT

PART I
Provision of Supplies

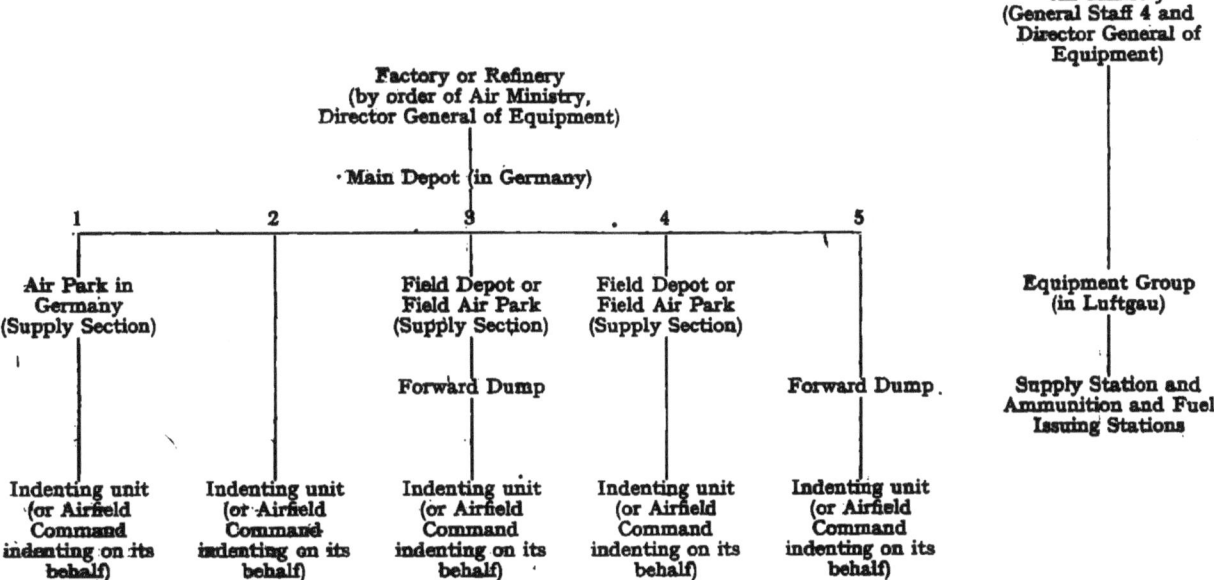

PART II
Provision of Aircraft Equipment

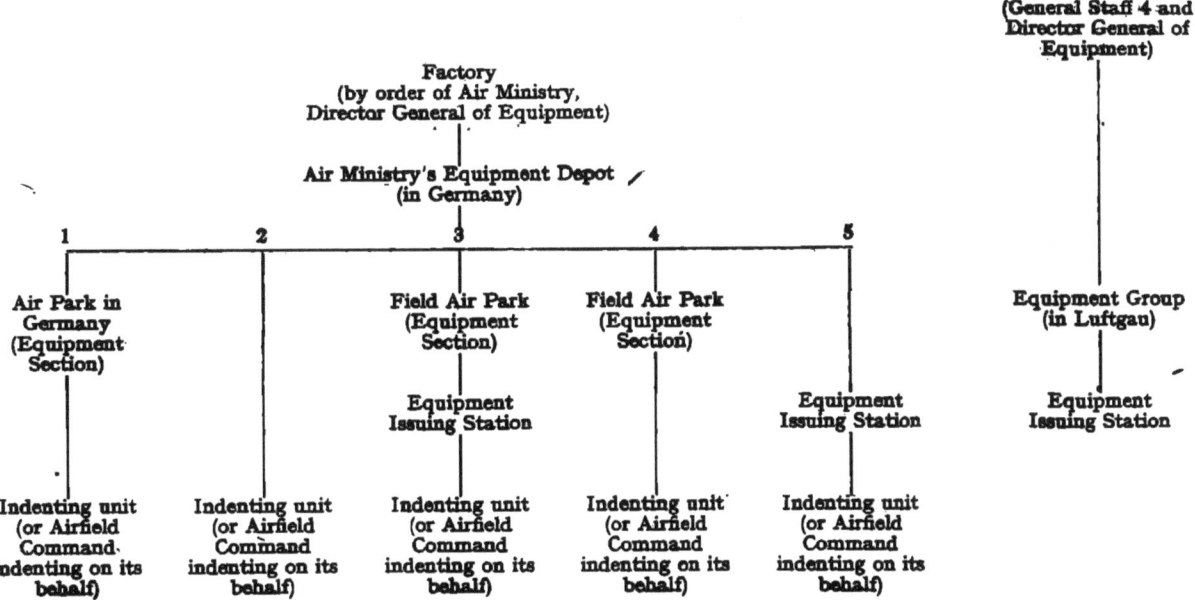

MAP 29

MAIN DEPOTS AND PARKS FOR AIRCRAFT AND EQUIPMENT
(January, 1943)

1. Depots

There are, in Germany, eight Air Ministry Equipment Depots (Luftzeugämter) for holding stocks of both aircraft and aircraft equipment, and arranging their delivery to units, through Airfield Commands, Air Parks, Equipment Issuing Stations, etc. Each depot specialises in particular types of aircraft, aircraft engines and often in particular types of equipment. In addition, they are main stores for most kinds of standard aircraft equipment. Their names and specialities are as follows:—

Depot	Chief types of aircraft stored	Aircraft engines stored	Special types of equipment stored
Erding	Me.109 ..	B.M.W.	—
Finow	Ju.87; Ju.88 ..	Bramo	Safety gear.
Koelleda	Hs.126; Hs.129; Do.17; Fi.156.	Jumo	Navigation, optical, hydraulic.
Liegnitz	Me.110; Me.210; FW.189; FW.190.	Bramo	Electrical.
Sagan-Kuepper	He.111; He.177	D.B.	—
Schwerin ..	Arado (Land) (Not for a/c)	Argus .. (Not for a/c engines).	Safety gear. Signals.
Teltow			
Travemuende	Sea-borne a/c.	Various	Sea and smoke.

There is also an Equipment Depot, for the East, at Warsaw.

It seems that shortly before the War one or two of these Equipment Depots were moved away from N.W. Germany, owing to its vulnerability. They were re-established in Silesia and East Germany. Originally, the sites were chosen and staffs provided under Luftgau auspices. But, when the Air Ministry decided that each should specialise in particular types of aircraft and engines, the sites were, as far as possible, allocated so as to be near the factories chiefly concerned.

2. Parks

Each Luftgau in Germany has an Air Park (Luftpark) (or two) for storing aircraft equipment for use in its area. Sometimes equipment is delivered through these Parks to the Field Air Parks on the battle-fronts. They are also sometimes used by the Air Ministry as subsidiaries to Equipment Depots for storing aircraft, also for acting as aircraft-supply-airfields to Operational Commands, and for carrying out re-equipment of flying units.

Principal Air Parks attached to home Luftgaus are as follows:—

L.G.I. Gutenfeld; L.G.II Posen; L.G.III Jueterbog; L.G.IV Delitzch; L.G.VI Paderborn; L.G.VII Gablingen; L.G.VIII Gleiwitz; L.G.XI Gardelegen; L.G.XII Nidda; L.G.XIII Illesheim; L.G.XVII Wiener Neustadt.

There is also one at Kiel for storing equipment of sea-borne aircraft.

There are shown on the map some additional Air Parks in or near Germany, e.g., Rotenburg, Anklam, Prossnitz and Metz.

Some half-dozen airfields in Germany are habitually used as Aircraft Distributing Stations. Gutersloh, for instance, has often been so used for Ju. 88s. Munchen/Riem has for a long time been used as a distributing centre for several types of aircraft destined for the Mediterranean area.

Field Air Parks are established in occupied countries so as to act as intermediate stores, between the main stores in Germany and the Equipment Issuing Stations and units at the front. Each "forward" Luftgau may have from one to four of these Parks, according to the varying factors of (i) territory to be covered, (ii) communications with Germany, (iii) number of units to be supplied. They are sometimes used as Aircraft Distributing Centres, and they are also kept as closely in touch as possible with the aircraft repair organisation, such as Front Repair Stations, set up in factories, and Field Workshops.

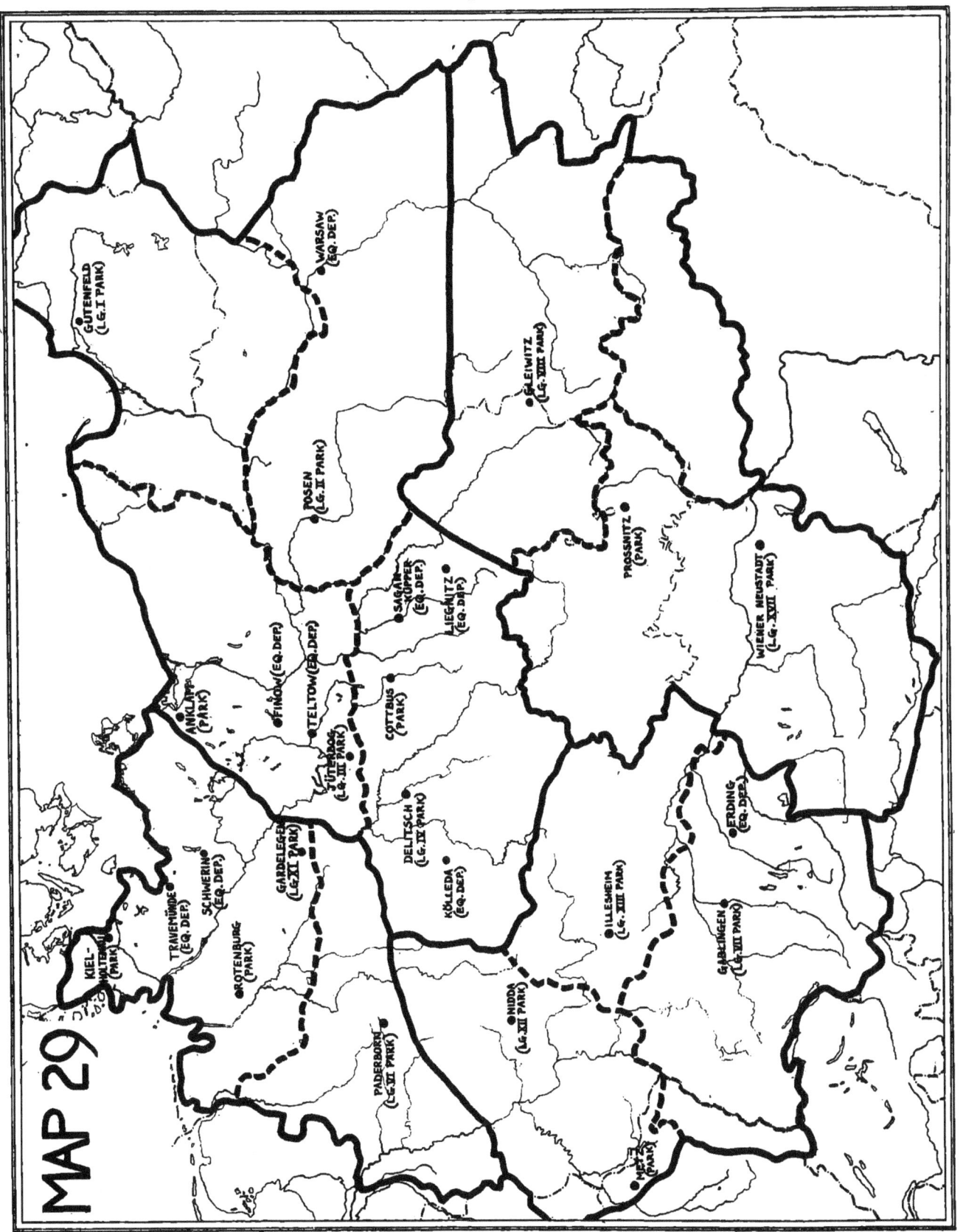

DIAGRAM 30

SIGNALS ORGANISATION

1. No small part of the success of G.A.F. operations in the early part of the War was due to the high degree of organisation of the signals service, which forms an integral part of the G.A.F. itself. In order to appreciate the organisation of this service it is necessary to realise that the following vital responsibilities are undertaken by it :—
   - (i) The transmission of all orders and communications, if possible both by land line (telephone and teleprinter) and by wireless telegraphy and telephony.
   - (ii) The establishment and supervision of all navigational aids such as W/T, D/F, Radio and visual beacons.
   - (iii) Observer Corps work in defence against air attack.
   - (iv) Control of traffic, air safety, and rescue services.
   - (v) Interception of enemy signals.

2. For this purpose the Luftflotten, Fliegerkorps and Luftgaus have their own signals regiments.

3. The regiments are formed of specialist companies, each dealing with a specific aspect of signals work. Each company has a number of platoons composed of detachments, or self-contained units specialising in the work for which the company caters.

4. These detachments have among others the following types of duties :—Servicing of telephones and teleprinters ; construction of telephone, teleprint and telegraph lines, and laying of field cables ; supervision of radio and visual beacons ; interception of enemy signals ; aircraft observation and reporting ; and liaison with the Army in close support.

5. In addition some regiments have signals aircraft, generally Ju. 52s, which act as advanced W/T and D/F Stations on the ground.

6. The duties of the Luftflotte and Fliegerkorps regiments are the laying of communications networks in their areas of operation, as newly occupied territory is taken over, and the erection and supervision of W/T and visual beacons and the like. In addition, one company of a Fliegerkorps regiment supplies the signals personnel allocated to the Air Liaison officers (or " Flivos ") for close support of the Army.

7. The Luftgau signals regiments, on the other hand, seeing that the Luftgau is responsible for the defence of its area against aerial attack, are composed almost entirely of companies specially organised for aircraft reporting and for manning the many Observer Corps and Radar posts.

8. Many Airfield Regional Commands in occupied territories have their own signals companies for organising the communication in their own districts. The platoons of the companies are allotted to the subordinate Airfield Commands.

9. Each Geschwader has a signals company in order to provide its subordinate Gruppen with signals platoons.

10. On an airfield which is occupied by an operational unit, there will, therefore, be two signals platoons, one belonging to the Airfield Command (or Luftgau side of the G.A.F.) and the other to the operational unit (Gruppe).

11. The airfield signals platoon is responsible for airfield telecommunications and exchanges, and for the following W/T services :—Airfield ground-to-ground communications and airfield safety service, i.e. reporting movements of aircraft, transmitting their positions and so on.

12. All tactical signals work is, however, carried out by the signals personnel of the operational unit, who maintain contact with the aircraft during operational flights.

13. In addition to the above-mentioned types of units there is a specialised regiment for experimental and research work on signals methods ; and the C.-in-C. of the G.A.F. has his own regiment.

14. A recent development has been the formation of special regiments to man the signals organisation for night-fighter defence. It is probable that each Fighter Division has its own signals regiment which would be used for manning and servicing the G.C.I. Stations.

15. A general plan of the G.A.F. Signals organisation is shown diagrammatically in Part I on the opposite page. Part II shows in diagrammatic form the composition of a typical Fliegerkorps Signals Regiment with its various specialist Companies.

DIAGRAM 30

PART I
SIGNALS ORGANISATION

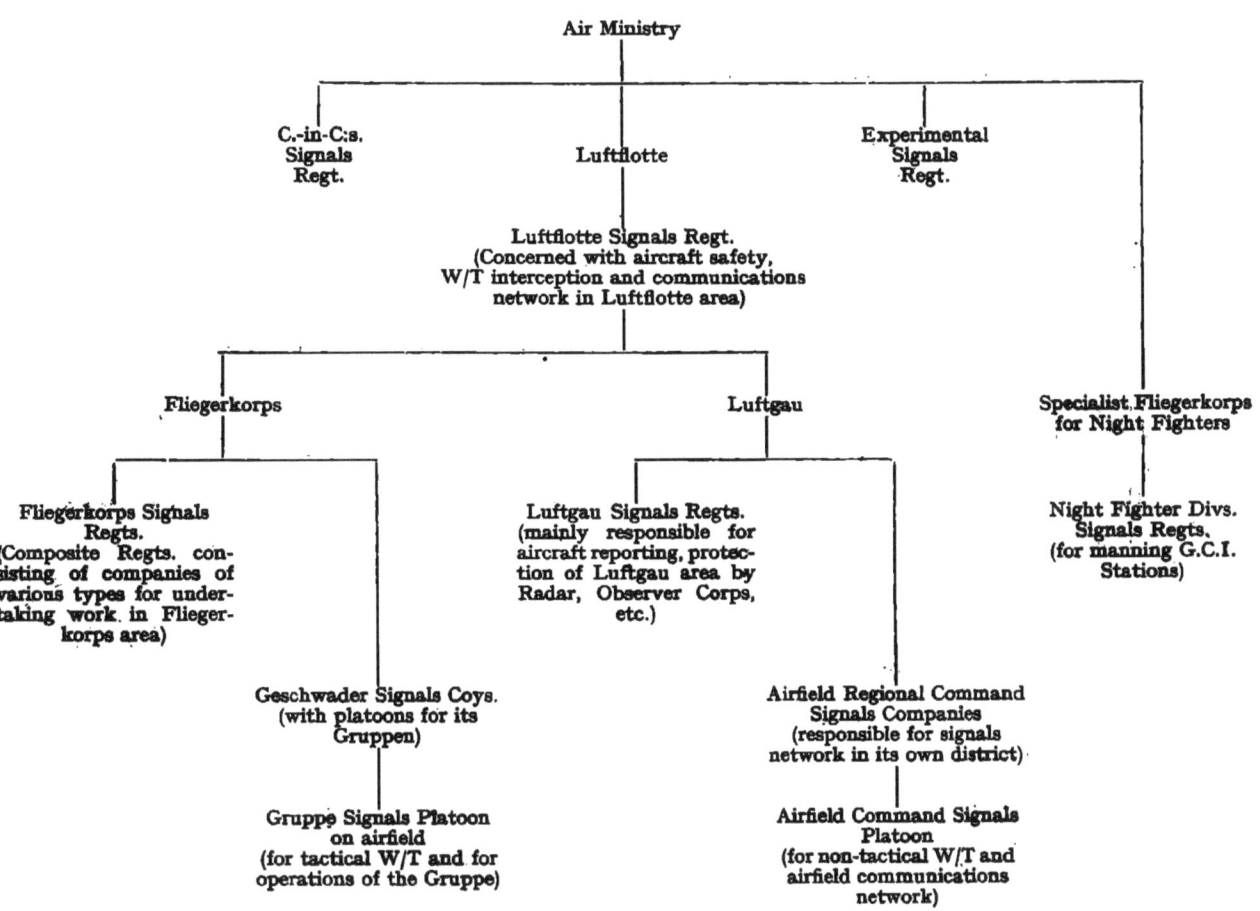

PART II
TYPICAL FLIEGERKORPS SIGNALS REGIMENT

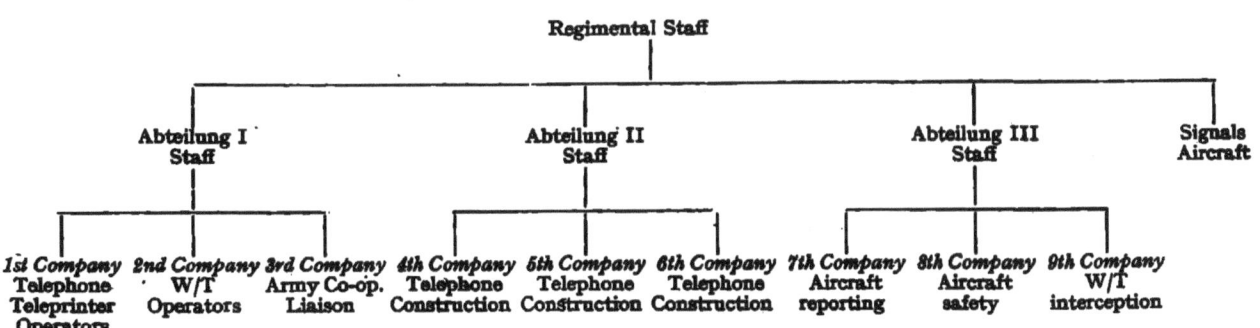

DIAGRAM 31

FLYING TRAINING, 1939-42

1. Germany started the War with a large reserve of trained crews.

2. Early in the War the training of fighter and bomber pilots ended at the specialist fighter and bomber schools respectively.

3. During the first year of the War the losses were not sufficient to absorb the flow of trained personnel coming out of the schools.

4. This led to the establishment of—
   (i) Operational Training Schools, probably early in 1940.
   (ii) Reserve Training Staffeln in the Autumn of 1940 (which eventually developed into the fourth (Reserve Training) Gruppen for all types of operational units during the first half of 1941).

5. During the Summer and Autumn of 1941, G.A.F. losses on the Russian front were heavy. The effects were first felt in the supply of fighter pilots; and, by February, 1942, the Reserve Training Gruppen of the fighter units had been abolished. A contraction to the Operational Training Pool arrangement resulted (see Fighter. (5) in diagram opposite).

6. During 1942 large numbers of Ju. 52s and He. 111s were withdrawn from the "C" Schools and Blind Flying Schools. There was also a shortage of aircraft fuel.

At that time the normal course of training for bomber crews had been—
   (i) "A/B" School (for elementary flying training, using elementary types).
   (ii) "C" Schools (for conversion to T/E types, using Ju. 52, He. 111, Do. 17).
   (iii) Blind Flying School (using Ju. 52).
   (iv) Bomber Specialist School (using He. 111 and Ju. 88).
   (v) Reserve Training Gruppen (using Ju. 88 and He. 111).
   (vi) Operational unit (using Ju. 88 and He. 111).

7. The withdrawal of aircraft from the "C" Schools and the Blind Flying Schools created a hiatus in training resulting in a surplus of partially trained crews in the early training schools and a lack of fully trained pupils ready to go into the Reserve Training Gruppen.

8. As a result the Bomber Specialist Schools were closed and the Reserve Training Gruppen have had to take over the functions of the Bomber Specialist Schools.

9. So great was the damage thus inflicted on the training programme that even operational units had to be used for training crews.

10. The diagram opposite illustrates the course of events described in the preceding paragraphs. On the right half of the diagram the quantity of reserves of personnel under operational training at the various stages is shown by black squares, the smallest of which represents a large Gruppe and the largest of which represents 16 Gruppen.

11. As, by the Autumn of 1942, the Reserve Training Gruppen were largely used to undertake the function of the abolished Bomber Schools, they are not shown as part of the reserve of personnel.

DIAGRAM 31

		PILOTS UNDER TRAINING				RESERVE OF PERSONNEL UNDER OPERATIONAL TRAINING		
FIGHTER	① 1939	A/B SCHOOLS		FIGHTER SCHOOLS		—	—	
	② EARLY 1940	A/B SCHOOLS		FIGHTER SCHOOLS		O.T. SCHOOL ■	—	
	③ LATE 1940	A/B SCHOOLS		FIGHTER SCHOOLS		—	R.T. STAFFELN ■	
	④ EARLY 1941	A/B SCHOOLS		FIGHTER SCHOOLS		—	R.T. GRUPPEN ■	
	⑤ EARLY 1942	A/B SCHOOLS		FIGHTER SCHOOLS		O.T. POOLS ■	—	

BOMBER	① 1939	A/B SCHOOLS	C SCHOOLS	BLIND FLYING SCHOOLS	BOMBER SCHOOLS	—	—	
	② EARLY 1940	A/B SCHOOLS	C SCHOOLS	BLIND FLYING SCHOOLS	BOMBER SCHOOLS	O.T. SCHOOLS ■	—	
	③ LATE 1940	A/B SCHOOLS	C SCHOOLS	BLIND FLYING SCHOOLS	BOMBER SCHOOLS	O.T. SCHOOLS ■	R.T. STAFFELN ■	
	④ EARLY 1941	A/B SCHOOLS	C SCHOOLS	BLIND FLYING SCHOOLS	BOMBER SCHOOLS	—	R.T. GRUPPEN ■	
	⑤ AUTUMN 1942	A/B SCHOOLS	C SCHOOLS	BLIND FLYING SCHOOLS		←- - - - - - -	R.T. GRUPPEN ■	

MAP 32

TRAINING UNITS USED FOR GROUND AND AIR DEFENCE, 1942

I.—Ground Defence

By the Spring of 1942 the German apprehensions regarding the opening of a second front in the West impelled them to strengthen their defences in that quarter. The Army units in the West were inadequate for all the calls to be made on them. In particular, the Army was unable to supply enough troops to protect the airfields. It was accordingly decided to move some 20 of the 30 or more Flying Training Regiments (Fliegerausbildungsregimenter) or Recruit Regiments (corresponding to our I.T.Ws.) from Germany, which was their standard situation, to Holland, Belgium and France so that they could be used for airfield defence and for the reinforcement of the Army generally.

The normal function of these Recruit Regiments was infantry and disciplinary training. The course in war-time lasted about three months. Each Regiment included some 1,500 to 3,000 recruits. When the move to the West was made their name was changed to Flying Regiments (Fliegerregimenter), doubtless to indicate the alteration in function.

One of these Regiments was, in fact, actively engaged in airfield defence during the Allied attack on Dieppe on 16th August, 1942.

The move of so large a number of training establishments from Germany (where most of the Flying Schools were situated) to the West must have caused some disorganisation in the training arrangements. It illustrates the extent of the shortage of ground troops as early as the Summer of 1942.

The moves of the 20 above-mentioned Recruit Regiments from their locations in Germany in 1940 to those in the West in 1942 are shown in the Map opposite. In a few instances there were moves from town to town in Germany during 1941.

Most of these Regiments, if not all, moved to Russia at the end of 1942 where the need for reinforcement was then even greater than in the West. They became incorporated in G.A.F. Field Divisions.

In addition to the Recruit Regiments, practically the whole of Parachute Division 7 (withdrawn from Russia in the Spring) was based in the Cherbourg area.

II.—Air Defence

In the Summer and Autumn of 1942, the G.A.F. had to provide emergency air defence in the West as a result of the expectation of invasion. It was only able to do this by moving units undertaking operational training.

The number of L.R.B. Reserve Training Gruppen (4th Gruppen) in the West was increased from 3 or 4 to 12 or 13 (out of a total of 17). Nearly all these were stationed at airfields near or a little South of Paris, suitably placed to cover most if not all the invasion danger-points.

Several of these Bomber Reserve Training Gruppen were occasionally engaged as operational units; and some in fact joined in the Baedeker raids on England in the Summer of 1942. But their main role was clearly defensive, so as to be prepared to attack Allied forces landing in the West.

In the early part of 1942 there were three Fighter Pools for operational training of fighters:—Fighter Pool South at Mannheim in Germany, Fighter Pool East at Krakau in Poland, and Fighter Pool West at Le Casaux in S.W. France. In the Autumn of 1942 the Pools at Mannheim and Krakau were moved to Villacoublay (near Paris) and St. Jean d'Angely in S.W. France respectively. The new location of these Pools in France was arranged so as to strengthen the fighter defences in the S.W. of France and to provide some additional strength in the North.

In the Map opposite, the locations of the L.R.B. Reserve Training Gruppen in the Summer and Autumn of 1942 are shown in large lettering, and that of the Fighter Pools in large lettering framed. There were three R.T. Gruppen at Orleans.

When the Germans occupied South France, as a result of the Allied landings in North Africa, the risk of further Allied landings was partly met by the move of many of the Training units from North to South France. Most of these units were moved back again after a few days, when the risk of landings in South France diminished.

The employment of the flying training units for defence must have had a disturbing effect on the courses of training.

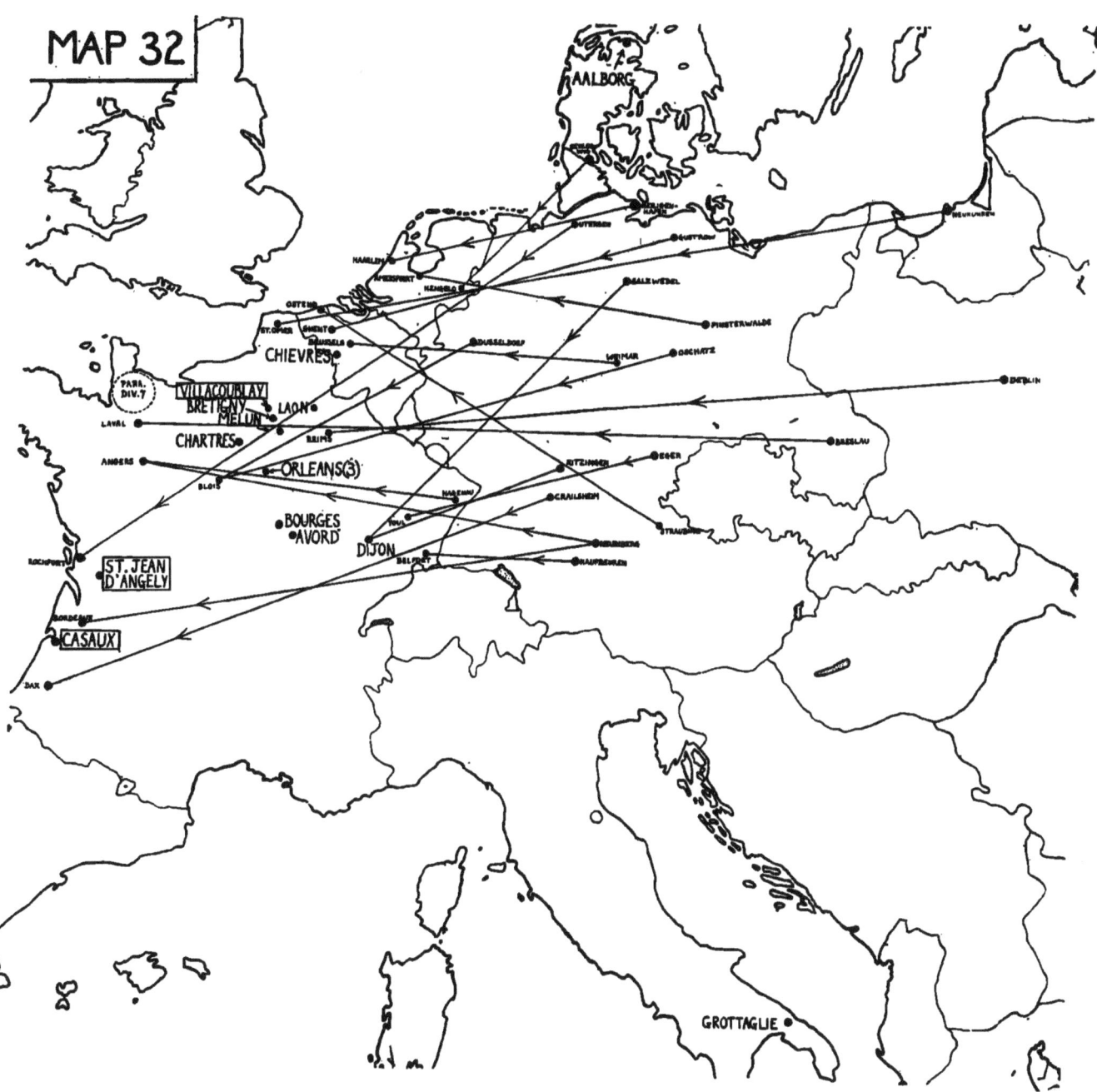

APPENDIX A

THE FUNCTIONS OF LUFTFLOTTE, FLIEGERKORPS AND LUFTGAU

1. (i) The *Luftflotte* is both an operational and an administrative Command, though these two sides of its activities can be regarded as distinct. It has an area assigned to it; and, in war-time, this area includes the new administrative districts set up in occupied countries.

(ii) For operational purposes the Luftflotte comprises one to three Fliegerkorps; and for administrative purposes it comprises one to three Luftgaus.

(iii) All Commands and formations below the Luftflotte are either essentially operational (i.e. Fliegerkorps, Geschwader, Gruppe, Staffel) or essentially for administration and supply (i.e. Luftgau and Airfield Command). But the Luftflotte is a vast organisation, amounting as it were to a local Air Force in itself. It consequently has not only a large Operations Department, but also a large Quartermaster's Department which is responsible for giving orders to its Luftgaus and Fliegerkorps regarding supplies of new aircraft and aircraft equipment, transport of supplies and equipment, and development of airfields. As the Luftflotte holds the reins of both operational and administrative activities, it is in a position to ensure that the two are kept in proper relation to each other.

2. (i) The *Fliegerkorps*, which is a purely operational Command, consists of a variable number of flying units of several different types. The number of units and the types depend on circumstances. Three hundred aircraft (or about 10 Gruppen) would constitute a small Fliegerkorps; and 720 aircraft (or about 24 Gruppen) would constitute a large one.

(ii) The most important part of the Fliegerkorps Headquarters is the Operations Department. Although it has a Quartermaster's Branch, the Fliegerkorps and its flying units depend in all main essentials on the Luftgau for administrative and supply services.

(iii) The Fliegerkorps is allotted a sector or an area of activities on a battle-front which is either coincident with or part of the area allotted to the "forward" Luftgau on which it depends for administration and supply. It may be moved from the area of one Luftflotte to that of another as the situation requires.

3. (i) The *Luftgau* in Germany is one of eleven G.A.F. administrative areas. Each Luftgau is sub-divided into about five regions (Airfield Regional Commands), and each Regional Command includes about five airfields administered by Operational Airfield Commands. A similar arrangement has been adopted in respect of occupied countries.

(ii) The Luftgau is responsible for (a) defence, especially by means of Flak, (b) airfield development, (c) signals installations (other than those for controlling operational flying units), (d) provision and transport of supplies (e.g. fuel and ammunition), (e) maintenance of aircraft and M/T (as opposed to light repairs), (f) accommodation, pay, clothing and rations, (g) training and recruiting in Germany.

(iii) The functions of Airfield Regional Commands are mentioned in Appendix C.

APPENDIX B

MOVES OF FLIEGERKORPS

(Reference should be made to Maps 3-11)

When it is said that a Fliegerkorps has moved from one battle-front to another, or from one sector to another, two different things may be meant. Sometimes the whole Fliegerkorps is moved, including the flying units. Sometimes merely the Headquarters Staff (with the necessary signals units) is moved, in order to take charge of a new set of flying units in its new area. Knowledge of the practice of the G.A.F. in such matters, namely the way in which the G.A.F. manipulates its operational Commands, helps in estimating the effect of future moves of Fliegerkorps.

In this connection emphasis must be laid on the contrast in kind between the Luftflotte Command and the Fliegerkorps Command. The Luftflotte, which normally controls one, two, or three Fliegerkorps, was, at the beginning of the War, a territorial Command with administrative jurisdiction over a fixed region, besides being also an operational Command. The four Luftflotten each had jurisdiction over a quarter of the Reich: No. 1 the N.E.; No. 2 the N.W.; No. 3 the S.W.; and No. 4 the S.E. This arrangement might have remained unaltered in the event of Germany fighting a defensive war. The spread of Germany's war of aggression, however, into territories outside the Reich has not only involved the extension outwards of the outer boundaries of the Luftflotte regions (e.g., Luftflotte 3 into the West, and Luftflotten 1 and 4 into the East); but, since the summer of 1941, Luftflotte 2 has had allotted to it battle regions far separate from its basic region in N.W. Germany—first in Russia and now in the Mediterranean. The G.A.F. is, in fact, prepared to detach Luftflotten from their basic regions if reasons of strategy so dictate. Furthermore, although a Luftflotte has jurisdiction over its battle region as it did over its basic one, most of the battle regions are constantly being expanded or contracted as campaigns are successful or otherwise. The Luftflotte, then, is still a territorial Command, but in a different sense from the original one.

On the other hand, the Fliegerkorps is primarily an operational Command. It is only a territorial one in a very limited sense. It had no administrative area in Germany like the Luftflotte, but merely a home base at a large city (Berlin, Dresden, Brunswick, Munich and Frankfurt). On the battle-fronts, the Fliegerkorps generally has a sector allotted to it. This arrangement is for operational purposes and does not imply administrative jurisdiction.

The Fliegerkorps has no standard establishment, either as regards the number or the types of the units which it comprises. Its composition is entirely flexible, based on the degree of importance and the character of its tasks. It may have a high proportion of long-range bombers if it is specially concerned with attacking communications or industrial targets, or it may have a high proportion of short-range aircraft if it is made responsible for the close support of an Army engaged in vital operations. The number of twin-engine fighters, reconnaissance aircraft, sea-borne aircraft, and so on vary considerably according to circumstances.

The average number of aircraft in a Fliegerkorps may be put at 450; but the number may be as small as 300 (exceptionally even 100) or may rise to 700 or even 800. A general impression of the extreme numbers of types of aircraft in a Fliegerkorps and the average numbers may be gained from the following tabular statement:—

	Low	High	Exceptionally High	Average
L.R.B.	60	270	330*	160
B.R.	30	60	90	45
D.B.	30	120	180	70
S.E.F.	60	120	210†	90
T.E.F.	0	60	120	30
A.C.	40	90	150	60
				455

* Fliegerkorps V, September, 1942.
† Fliegerkorps VIII, September, 1942.

When a Fliegerkorps is to be moved with its headquarters and also its flying units, the personnel involved may number about 15,000–20,000. If the move is one of several hundred miles, railway transportation will be chiefly used; and some 60 to 80 trains will be required, ordered to run, at say, 15 a day. (Much of the space will be occupied by M/T and equipment.) Under most favourable circumstances, therefore, a whole Fliegerkorps might complete such a move within a week. This short period would not allow time for the re-equipment and replacements generally necessary on such occasions.

In the event of a short move of, say, 200 miles, most of the transportation would be by road.

When a Fliegerkorps headquarters (with necessary signals units) only is moving, about 3,000 personnel and about 12 railway trains are involved; and the time taken by the move might be as short as two or three days. If the distance to be traversed is only 200–300 miles, the move could be effected entirely by means of M/T. The signals units are fully motorised.

It sometimes happens that a Fliegerkorps headquarters moving from one front or sector to another calls at its home base, or specially designated base in the Reich, so as to undergo re-organisation. This course would obviously involve delay. Instances of such calls are that of Fliegerkorps II at its home base at Dresden on its way from Russia to the Mediterranean in November, 1941, and those of Fliegerkorps VIII at its special base at Vienna twice in 1942 when making moves on the Russian front.

If several whole Fliegerkorps are moved together from one front to another distant one, the operation must clearly occupy considerably longer than a week. When Fliegerkorps II, IV and V were moved from the West to the Russian front in June, 1941, the time taken was just under three weeks; but, doubtless, this period included some necessary re-equipment on the way. Units of these Fliegerkorps were operating in the West in the first week of June and were ready for the Russian offensive on 22nd June (see Maps 5 and 6).

APPENDIX B—continued

Fliegerkorps VIII also had to be moved at the same time, from Greece to the Russian front. Some of its units were operating over Crete at the end of May and started to move early in June. This move, therefore, also occupied rather less than three weeks. Such a considerable period, for one Fliegerkorps, was due not only to a difficult railway journey, but also to a large amount of re-equipment *en route*, owing to recent intensive operations. Flying units were sent to special re-equipment bases behind their new operational area before proceeding to the front.

Usually the move of a Fliegerkorps, complete with units, has to be made with all possible speed, if for no other reason than that it must be left to the last moment in the interest of secrecy. It would certainly have been convenient to the G.A.F. to have moved some of the Fliegerkorps from the West to the East in May, 1941, instead of all of them (with the exception of one headquarters to be mentioned presently) in June. But such an early move would have disclosed the intention of an attack on Russia.

Sometimes, however, it has been practicable to undertake the move of a complete Fliegerkorps in a deliberate manner. For instance, the move of Fliegerkorps VIII from the West to the Balkans, preliminary to the attack on Greece in April, 1941, started at the beginning of the year, the infiltration into Rumania proceeding steadily in the expectation that the objective, though it might be guessed, would not be definitely disclosed.

When Fliegerkorps move complete with units, the operational aircraft are, as far as possible, flown to the new area, intermediate landing grounds and necessary accommodation *en route* being planned. It is often arranged for units which have been re-equipping in view of a projected move to fly their aircraft to the new area either from Germany or from a specially allotted area for re-equipment nearer the battle-front. Sometimes a Luftflotte is allotted a re-equipment area behind its battle-front and nearer to it than Germany.

In order to organise the arrangements for moves, a Fliegerkorps may have a special Planning Staff situated at its base headquarters in the Reich or at some other important centre conveniently placed in the circumstances. Such a Planning Staff is concerned in questions of re-equipment, especially of aircraft and M/T, and in questions of supplies, in so far as a Fliegerkorps is responsible for supplies, e.g. in respect of short-range units who may not be able to rely on the Luftgau organisation. It will also make arrangements with the Luftgau authorities in the new area regarding the accommodation, stores, etc., which will be required by its flying units.

Since the opening of the German offensive against Russia there have been several clear examples of the two classes into which the moves of Fliegerkorps fall. As remarked above, some of the moves have been those of the Fliegerkorps headquarters together with its flying units; others have been those of Fliegerkorps headquarters only, with such signals units as the occasion required. The short description of these examples in the following paragraphs is intended to give a general impression of the practice of the G.A.F.

In order to assist in clarifying what must necessarily be rather a complicated description, a tabular statement, showing the relative positions of Fliegerkorps at intervals between June, 1941, and December, 1942, is added to this article as Annex I. Some assistance may also be obtained by reference to Annex II which shows, in tabular form, the Luftflotten to which the various Fliegerkorps have been subordinated from time to time since the Battle of France.

In December, 1940, there were six Fliegerkorps headquarters on the Western front—more than were required in the winter months, especially in view of the decision, already made, to attack Greece and Russia in 1941. In January, 1941, the headquarters of Fliegerkorps VIII was moved from the West to Bucharest, and its units were gradually collected in the Balkans until they were ready for the attack on Greece in April, 1941.

In February, 1941, the headquarters of Fliegerkorps I, which could easily be spared from the West, was moved to its home base in East Prussia so that it might make preparations for the Russian campaign in the summer. Its units were left behind in the West. They were not yet required on the Eastern front; and their presence there would certainly have raised apprehensions in the Russians.

When most of the flying units in the West were quickly moved and concentrated on the Russian front in June, 1941, many of those which had been under Fliegerkorps I in the West were again subordinated to it.

Fliegerkorps II, IV and V, which remained complete in the West, were moved, with their units, to the Russian front at the latest possible stage, namely, in June, 1941. There was some re-assortment of units, as is natural in such a vast transfer of forces; and some units which had been re-equipping in Germany were allotted to Fliegerkorps as they arrived on the Russian Front.

When Fliegerkorps VIII made its move from Greece to the Russian front in June, it took nearly all its units with it, only leaving one or two to be transferred to Fliegerkorps X which had been operating in the Mediterranean and was moving its headquarters from Sicily to Greece.

Fliegerkorps VIII's first position on the Russian front was in the Northern part of the central sector; but, in August, 1941, when the Germans were to attempt an intensive drive on Leningrad, this Fliegerkorps, with its units, was moved into the Northern sector, adjoining its original one, so as to co-operate with Fliegerkorps I under Luftflotte 1 (see Appendix A). As soon as the drive on Leningrad had expended itself and the Germans had decided, at the end of September, to mount a massive attack on Moscow, Fliegerkorps VIII was moved back again, with its units, to its first position on the Russian front. These moves were short and easy ones, simply involving a transfer into the contiguous area of the adjoining Luftflotte Command and back again (see Map 6).

By November, 1941, the G.A.F. decided that there was need for a Luftflotte Command in the Mediterranean, where Fliegerkorps X had been operating with rather inadequate forces, as an independent Command directly under the Air Ministry. It was also decided that there must be two Fliegerkorps operating in the Mediterranean instead of one. Accordingly, Luftflotte 2 was taken from the Central Russian front with one of its two Fliegerkorps, namely, Fliegerkorps II, in order to strengthen the G.A.F. in the Mediterranean. This move of Fliegerkorps II was merely that of its headquarters. The majority of the units which had been under its command in Russia were transferred to Fliegerkorps VIII, which was left to hold the whole sector for which Luftflotte 2 (with its two Fliegerkorps) had previously been responsible. Not only single-engine fighters but long-range bombers were also left

APPENDIX B—continued

behind. A few of the units of Fliegerkorps II went to Germany to re-equip, but these returned to Russia. Fliegerkorps II's new units in the Mediterranean were collected from several quarters, from Germany (re-equipped units), some from Russia and one or two from Fliegerkorps X, already in the Mediterranean (see Map 7).

In April, Fliegerkorps VIII's headquarters was taken from the Moscow front, for which it had been responsible as an independent Command directly under the Air Ministry, and despatched, without its units, to the Crimea so as to control the units on the Southern front which were concentrated there for the subjection of the peninsula prior to the summer offensive. Fliegerkorps VIII received by way of addition to the units which it took over in the South some further units which had been re-equipped in Germany or elsewhere.

At the same time, the headquarters of Fliegerkorps V was sent to the central front to take under its command most of the units which had been operating under Fliegerkorps VIII (see Map 8).

When Fliegerkorps VIII had completed its task in the Crimea, its headquarters was moved to the Kursk front in June, 1942, for the attack with which the summer offensive was to open. Only a few changes were made in the positions of flying units. The headquarters of Fliegerkorps VIII and the headquarters of Fliegerkorps IV must have merely changed places, each taking over, substantially, the units previously in charge of the other (see Map 9).

It will be seen that these moves of the headquarters of Fliegerkorps VIII, first to the Crimea and then to the Kursk sector, were not moves of Fliegerkorps in the full sense. They were merely moves of its headquarters staff which was evidently considered the most efficient to undertake the support of important attacks by the Army. The headquarters of Fliegerkorps VIII had gained a reputation for specialising in the technique of close support; and it was paid the compliment of being selected and posted to take charge of the units already stationed in the critical sectors, with the addition of some supplementary close support units.

It may be remarked, parenthetically, that, from the early stages in the Russian campaign, the G.A.F. had never enough single-engine fighter and dive-bomber units to provide close support for all parts of the long front at the same time. Close support units had to be moved from sector to sector so as to form a sufficient concentration of them at the place and time at which the Army was making its main thrust. Several of these units were moved, on this principle, to the Leningrad front in August, 1941, for the encirclement of Kiev in September, 1941, to the Moscow front in October, 1941, and to the Black Sea area at the end of October, 1941 (see Map 19). About 90 dive-bombers and 80-90 single-engine fighters which were lent to Luftflotte 2 by Luftflotte 4 for the Moscow offensive in October were sent back to Luftflotte 4 in the South for the drive towards Rostov and the attack on the Crimea in November. Other examples could be given, such as the move of close support units from the Donetz sector to the Crimea for the attack on Sebastopol in January, 1942.

If the military situation on a sector of the battle-front requires that the number of flying units shall be largely and rapidly increased, the object is sometimes effected, not by moving a complete Fliegerkorps, but by setting up an ad hoc Command to which units of all the main types are moved from other sectors or from reserve. This happened in the Donetz sector at the end of 1942, when it was urgently necessary to concentrate strong air forces in an attempt to stem the Russian advance in that sector. Alternatively, a simpler method may be adopted; and the strength of flying units under a Fliegerkorps may be rapidly raised to meet a new or intensified offensive by opposing forces without the addition of an ad hoc subsidiary Command to the Fliegerkorps. For instance, in December, 1942, when the Russians were making a promising attack in the Don sector, Fliegerkorps I's headquarters (which had been moved to that sector from the North in July, 1942, and had had a small force put under it, as G.A.F. Command Don) was evidently given a quick addition of about 140 aircraft. These came chiefly from Fliegerkorps IV in the Caucasus, from which area it was easiest to spare them. In this way G.A.F. Command Don was assisted in its effort to meet a dangerous situation by having the number of its aircraft raised from about 100 (an exceptionally low figure) to about 240 (see Maps 10 and 11).

When Fliegerkorps I was moved away from the command of Luftflotte 1 in the North in July, 1942, Luftflotte 1 was left without any Fliegerkorps under it, a very unusual arrangement. But it still retained under its command the units which had been controlled by Fliegerkorps I (see Map 11). It is presumed that some special staff was established so as to avoid the Staff Officers of the Luftflotte suffering the indignity of direct communication with flying units.

Besides the abundance of evidence of the ease and frequency with which flying units are moved from Fliegerkorps to Fliegerkorps, we also have ample evidence of the common practice of moving Fliegerkorps headquarters to take over entirely new sets of flying units in new sectors. All this information serves to emphasise the changing character of the composition of a normal Fliegerkorps—a situation which must result in a low *esprit de Fliegerkorps* among the flying units.

The moves of Fliegerkorps from one Luftflotte to another are less frequent than moves within a Luftflotte area. Since the beginning of the Russian campaign in 1941, Fliegerkorps IV has been continuously under Luftflotte 4. Fliegerkorps II has remained under Luftflotte 2. Other Fliegerkorps have changed their subordination at least once. Fliegerkorps VIII has changed it three times (see Annex II).

It should be added that Luftflotte 5 was created as a new command for the North after the occupation of Norway. For some seven months this Luftflotte had Fliegerkorps X under its command; but, since the end of 1941 (when Fliegerkorps X went to the Mediterranean), it has been without a Fliegerkorps Command and has had Fliegerfuehrers to control the flying units. The setting-up of Luftflotte 5 and the changes in its composition further illustrate the way in which the basic notions regarding Luftflotten and their subordinate Fliegerkorps have been modified under war conditions.

ANNEX I

CHANGING POSITIONS OF FLIEGERKORPS ON THE RUSSIAN FRONT
(June, 1941 to January, 1943)

June–July, 1941—
- Luftflotte 1 — Fliegerkorps I — Towards Leningrad.
- Luftflotte 2 { Fliegerkorps VIII, Fliegerkorps II } Towards Moscow.
- Luftflotte 4 { Fliegerkorps V — Towards Kiev.; Fliegerkorps IV — S. Russia. }

August–September, 1941—
- Luftflotte 1 { Fliegerkorps I, Fliegerkorps VIII } Leningrad front.
- Luftflotte 2 — Fliegerkorps II — Moscow front.
- Luftflotte 4 { Fliegerkorps V — Towards Kiev and Kharkov.; Fliegerkorps IV — S. Russia. }

October–November, 1941—
- Luftflotte 1 — Fliegerkorps I — Leningrad front.
- Luftflotte 2 { Fliegerkorps VIII, Fliegerkorps II } Moscow front.
- Luftflotte 4 { Fliegerkorps V — Kharkov front.; Fliegerkorps IV — S. Russia and Crimea. }

December, 1941—
- Luftflotte 1 — Fliegerkorps I — Leningrad front.
- None — Fliegerkorps VIII — Moscow front.
- Luftflotte 4 { Fliegerkorps V — Don front and S. Russia.; Fliegerkorps IV — Crimea. }

January–March, 1942—
- Luftflotte 1 — Fliegerkorps I — Leningrad front.
- None — Fliegerkorps VIII — Moscow front.
- Luftflotte 4 { Fliegerkorps IV — Don front and S. Russia.; Fliegerkorps V — Crimea. }

April–May, 1942—
- Luftflotte 1 — Fliegerkorps I — Leningrad front.
- None — Command East (V) — Moscow front.
- Luftflotte 4 { Fliegerkorps IV — Don front and S. Russia.; Fliegerkorps VIII — Crimea. }

June, 1942—
- Luftflotte 1 — Fliegerkorps I — Leningrad front.
- None — Command East (V) — Moscow front.
- Luftflotte 4 { Fliegerkorps VIII — Kursk and Don fronts.; Fliegerkorps IV — S. Russia and Crimea. }

July, 1942–January, 1943—
- Luftflotte 1 — None — Leningrad front.
- None — Command East (V) — Moscow front.
- None — Command Don (I) — Don front.
- Luftflotte 4 { Fliegerkorps VIII — Stalingrad front.; Fliegerkorps IV — Caucasus front. }

ANNEX II

SUBORDINATION OF FLIEGERKORPS TO LUFTFLOTTEN

	May 1940	July 1940	Sept. 1940	Jan. 1941	June 1941	Aug. 1941	Oct. 1941	Dec. 1941	Jan. 1942	Apr. 1942	July 1942
Fliegerkorps I	2	2	2	?1	1	1	1	1	1	1	Indep.
Fliegerkorps II	3	2	2	2	2	2	2	2	2	2	2
Fliegerkorps IV	2	3	3	3	4	4	4	4	4	4	4
Fliegerkorps V	3	3	3	3	4	4	4	4	4	Indep.	Indep.
Fliegerkorps VIII	3	3	2	4	2	1	2	Indep.	Indep.	4	4
Fliegerkorps IX	2	2	2	2	3	3	3	3	3	3	3
Fliegerkorps X	5	5	5	Indep.	Indep.	Indep.	Indep.	2	2	2	2

NOTE.—The arabic numerals are those of the Luftflotten to which the Fliegerkorps were subordinate.

APPENDIX C

AIRFIELD COMMANDS

Summary of Functions

1. *The Airfield Regional Command* is a staff (with about 100 personnel) in charge of supply and administration in one of several regions of a Luftgau. It stands between the Luftgau and the Operational Airfield Commands. Its main function is to superintend the activities of its Operation Airfield Commands (of which there are from, say, three to eight, according to circumstances).

2. The subjects in respect of which an Airfield Regional Command exercises superintendence over Operational Airfield Commands are as follows :—
   (i) Serviceability and development of airfields, including the provision of accommodation (Superintendence is, in this respect, partly effected through a Field Works Office).
   (ii) Defence of airfields.
   (iii) Repair of aircraft and M/T.
   (iv) Provision of spare parts and equipment.
   (v) Storage and delivery of supplies (including provision of rations).
   (vi) Signals communications.

3. The Airfield Regional Command has attached to it and to some extent under its charge a set of maintenance and supply units. These units are centrally controlled in the Airfield Region in order to provide services to the airfields (and flying units on them) which the airfields cannot undertake themselves. The following units are normally attached to an Airfield Regional Command :—
   (i) Field Workshop Platoon—for repair of aircraft.
   (ii) M/T Repair Platoon—for repair of M/T.
   (iii) Equipment Issuing Station—for storage and distribution of local stocks of equipment for aircraft and M/T.
   (iv) Supply Station—for managing local fuel, ammunition and ration dumps.
   (v) Supply Company—for operating local dumps and depots.
   (vi) Transport Columns and Fuel Columns—for transporting supplies.

4. In order that it may carry out its responsibilities in regard to signals communications, the Airfield Regional Command has a Signals Company, the platoons of which are distributed over the Operational Airfields. In this connection, the Airfield Regional Command has to see that the Air Movement Controls in its region are efficiently operated.

5. The Airfield Regional Command includes an office for dealing with the personnel under its charge and superintendence. This personnel may amount to as many as 3,000. The Officer Commanding is usually an Oberst (Colonel).

6. *The Operational Airfield Command* is a staff which has the practical task of administering and supplying an airfield. If an airfield is a fairly important one, a whole staff is used. If less important, a detachment of a staff is used. Some flying units with short-range aircraft have to look after the administration and supply of their airfields themselves, especially when a battle-front is in a fluid state. They have extra personnel for the purpose.

7. The functions of an Operational Airfield Command are as follows :—
   (i) Maintenance of serviceability and development of the airfield. The Command usually has attached to it a Works Superintendent's Office with about thirty technicians and also a Company of a Works Battalion. (A whole Battalion (750 strong) may be attached, if necessary.) The Works Superintendent and the Works Company also undertake building, heating, water supply and similar activities. Reports on the serviceability of the airfield, including, for instance, effects of enemy air raids, are passed by W/T to higher authority, and are disseminated on the appropriate signals network.
   (ii) Provision of accommodation and rations to the flying units using the airfield.
   (iii) Defence of the airfield. The Operational Airfield Command provides personnel for guard duties from the Airfield Company and, in some instances, from an attached Land Defence Platoon. Flak units are also attached. The senior officer commanding any flying unit on the airfield controls the Commandant of the Operational Airfield Command in regard to defence.
   (iv) Signals communications (telephone, teleprinter, W/T). These are undertaken by the Signals Platoon allotted as mentioned in para. 4 above. There is an Air Movement Control at each Operational Airfield Command. The Operational Airfield Command has nothing to do with the signals installations necessary for controlling aircraft on operations. This work is undertaken by the tactical W/T Station manned by the Signals Platoon of the flying unit.
   (v) Repairs of aircraft and M/T. Such repairs as are beyond the ability of the flying unit are undertaken by the Operational Airfield Command, if practicable, or sent back to the Airfield Regional Command or even further, if the repairs are heavy.
   (vi) Provision of spare parts and equipment. Indents put forward by flying units will be satisfied either from the stocks of the local Equipment Issuing Station or from a Field Air Park further back.
   (vii) Storage and delivery of supplies. The Operational Airfield Command keeps stores of fuel, bombs and ammunition which are replenished from local dumps and depots or from main depots.
   (viii) Provision of Meteorological, Medical and Welfare services. There are sections for these.

8. The average strength in personnel of an Operational Airfield Command, inclusive of the Signals Platoon, but exclusive of other attached units, is 350. It is most frequently commanded by a Major; but the rank of the Commandant can be equivalent to that of Captain or Lieut.-Colonel.

APPENDIX D

PARTICULARS OF GROUND ORGANISATION IN NORTH AFRICA (March, 1943)

LUFTGAU TUNIS

Airfield Regional Commands	BIZERTA	TUNIS	SOUSSE	SFAX	GABES	No. of Units Ostr Luftgau Stab.	Average per Unit	Total
Airfield Commands and Detachments		A.R.C. TUNIS—5/XIII (Trop.) Bizerta—Sidi Ahmed—B29/III (Trop.) Tunis—El Aouina—E.85/IV Maffe de Zit (Detachment) Kairostat		A.R.C. SFAX—18/XI (Trop.) La Smala—E29/III (Trop.) El Djem (Detachment) La Falconnerie—E23/VII (Trop.) Sfax—E20/VI (Trop.) Mezzouna—South (Detachment) Mezzouna—North (Def. C.1/VII)	A.R.C. GABES—10/III (Trop.) Oudref Fatgases—E6/IV (Trop.) Mataltiq (Detachment) Gabes-West—E1/III (Trop.) Gabes-East (Detachment)	3 7	100 300	600 300 2,100
Supplies								
Main Supply Stations	"Dosier"	2/VII (Trop.)	1/VII (Trop.)	"Sfax"	Patt 2/XI	4	50	200
Supply Companies	1/XII; 14/XI (Trop.); 14/IV	13/VI (Trop.); H.G.18/IV	7/III (Trop.)	1/XI (Trop.); Patt 2/XI		8	250	2,000
Supply Platoons	4/VII	5/VII	—	—	—	2	60	120
Field Ammunition Depots	8/VI	—	—	—	1/IV	1	50	50
Munition Issuing Stations		6/VII	19/VII (Trop.)	—	—	3	50	150
Field a/c. fuel Depots	1/VII (Trop.); 2/VII (Trop.)	z.b.V.1/VIII	—	—	4/VI	3	50	150
A/C fuel issuing station		3/VI (Mot.)	—	—	5/VI (Mot.)	1	50	50
Supply Column Staff	—	22/IV; 17/IV; 58/IV (Trop.); 31/XVII (Trop.)	—	—	—	2	50	100
Transport Columns	85/XI; 33/XII	z.b.V. Stab. 1, 7 & 8 Coys.	—	—	89/XI; 5/XI; 15/XII	9	40	360
Fuel Columns M/T. Regt. Speer	—	—	—	3 & 4 Coys.	502/XIII; 508/VII	3	80	240
Air Equipment and Repair								
British Air Park	—	Tunis—"Africa"—7/XII (Trop.)	—	—		3	100	300
Equipment Issuing Stations	—	Tunis—4/I and 103/IV (Mot.)	S. of Sfax—1/VII (Trop.)		Gabes (Branch Station)	1	300	300
Heavy Field Workshop Abt.	—					1	100	100
Light Field Workshop Abt.	—	Bizerta—Kairouba—IV/20	25 km. S. of Sousse—1/30			1	100	100
Workshop Platoons	—	El Aouina—1/30; Kairouan—Eig. "Africa"	La Fauconnerie—2/30; Sfax-West—8/30			4	50	200
M/T. Equipment and Repair								
M/T. Equipment Issuing Station	—	Tunis—9/VII	"Sousse" Mahdia—10/VIII		Gabes (Branch of "Sousse")	3	40	120
M/T. Workshop Platoons	—	Tunis—z.b.V. and 108/VII	Sousse—4/III (Trop.) and Regt. Speer; Sfax 4/IV (Trop.) (Mot.); Gabes 3/XI (Mot.).l.			5	50	250
Signals								
Special Companies	—	Tunis—L.N. Komp. z.b.V. 5/XIII and Teleph. Telegr. Coy. ; Sousse—Luftgau Signals Company.				3	120	360
Salvage, Servicing, etc.								
A/C. Salvage Staff	—	Tunis—Luftzeugstab.108 (with 2 a/c. Salvage Platoons)	Sfax—3rd Platoon of 5 z.b.V.			1	270	270
Airfield Servicing Company	—	Tunis—5 z.b.V. and det. for Ju.52.	Sfax—3/VII			1	150	150
Repair Workshop for ground apparatus							50	50
Medical								
Medical Detachment	—		10 km. East of El Djem—2/IV (Mot.)			1	40	40
Flying Medical Detachment	—		9 km. S. of Sfax—Udls No. 2			1	20	20
Medical Park	—	Tunis—Branch Park (Mot.) 21				1	100	100
Laboratory	—		Sfax—G.A.F. Field Laboratory No. 1			1	10	10
Works								
Works Offices	—	Sfax—Stab. 21/XI; La Fauconnerie 2 and 3 Coys. of 21/XI				1	100	100
Works Battalion							550	550
								8,340

APPENDIX E

FLYING UNITS AND THEIR MOBILITY

Remarks regarding the mobility of flying units in the G.A.F. are prefaced here with short particulars of flying formations from the Staffel upwards.

1. (i) *The Staffel*, with nine aircraft, is the lowest in the grades of flying formations in so far as organisation is concerned.

(ii) Three Staffeln make up a Gruppe.

(iii) The Staffel has a Staffelkapitän and also an officer who acts as Adjutant. Members of the flying personnel supervise the technical, signals, and navigation branches as spare-time jobs.

(iv) The Staffel has aircraft allotted to it and the use of M/T from the establishment of the parent Gruppe. It often has a mobile repair shop of its own for light repairs to aircraft. The need for dispersal on airfields renders this inevitable.

(v) The numbers of the flying personnel of the Staffel vary from about 10 (for single-engine fighters) to 40 (for long-range bombers); and the ground personnel from about 150 (for S.E.Fs.) to 80 (for L.R.Bs.). The L.R.Bs. have smaller ground staffs because much of their servicing and administration is done for them by attached units or by airfield staffs.

2. (i) The *Gruppe* is in fact the standard or basic flying unit both for operational and administrative purposes. One Gruppe is normally based on each airfield. When orders are given for moves of flying units, the recipients are generally Gruppen. Although the Staffel is occasionally detached from its parent Gruppe for operational purposes, the three Staffeln of a Gruppe are usually based at the same airfield.

(ii) The Gruppe has 27 aircraft, plus 3 for the Gruppe Staff, making 30 in all.

(iii) It has a Kommandeur, Adjutant, Operations Officer (who may be responsible for navigation or signals), Technical Officer, and Medical Officer. It has a Signals Platoon. It seems that there is not always a whole-time Intelligence Officer.

(iv) The numbers of the flying personnel vary from about 35 (for S.E.Fs.) to 150 (for L.R.Bs.); and the ground personnel from about 515 (for S.E.Fs.) to 300 (for L.R.Bs.). The reason for the smaller ground staff for L.R.Bs. is given in sub-para. (v) of the preceding paragraph.

3. (i) The *Geschwader* normally comprises three Gruppen. It was evidently intended, at the time when the G.A.F. was planned, that the three Gruppen in a Geschwader should operate together on adjacent airfields. As, however, the G.A.F. has had to send units to an increasing number of battle-fronts, and as a result of withdrawals of Gruppen from operations and their subsequent despatch to new fronts, this arrangement has to some extent broken down. Still, the Geschwader organisation appears to be fully maintained, though its usefulness must necessarily be impaired. The Geschwader Staff remains in being even when its Gruppen are far separated.

(ii) The Geschwader Staff consists of a Kommodore, Adjutant, Operations Officer, Organisation Officer, Intelligence Officer, Navigation Officer, Technical Officer, Signals Officer, and sometimes M/T Officer, Photographic Officer and Meteorological Officer.

(iii) There are three aircraft for the Geschwader Staff, except in the case of S.E.Fs., when there are six.

Flying units cannot move to newly created fronts, or to an existing front, or from one part of an existing front to another, without preparation for their accommodation being made by the Luftgau (administration and supply) side of the G.A.F. If the move is to a new front, Luftgau Commands and units must be sent ahead. If the move is to an existing front the Luftgau Commands and units at and near the airfields concerned will often be able to accommodate an increased number of flying units until it is possible to reinforce the ground organisation. In these latter circumstances, transfer of flying units can be rapidly arranged.

The Airfield Commands (whose functions are mentioned in Appendix C) are the main channels of the Luftgau organisation through which flying units are accommodated, fed, supplied and obtain maintenance facilities. These Commands (or detachments of them) are always detailed to look after long-range flying units and sometimes short-range flying units; but, if a battle-front is in a state of flux, short-range flying units have to fend for themselves. This is not such a hardship as might appear, as they have extra personnel and M/T for the purpose; and, although they may have to fetch their ammunition, fuel and rations in their own M/T, the Luftgau organisation gives them all the help it can. Flak will be attached to them for defence. Special motorised Equipment Issuing Stations and Field Workshops are provided to assist short-range units to undertake repair and maintenance of aircraft.

A long-range bomber Gruppe moves in the main by rail. Only its key technical personnel and equipment move by air transport. It has, therefore, only about 20 M/T.

Short-range units, on the other hand, have about 100–130 M/T and are thus capable of moving entirely by means of their own M/T, though a long journey of several hundred miles will often be undertaken by rail. Air transport is used for some personnel when the move is urgent.

L.R.Bs., T.E.Fs. and D.Bs. have Airfield Servicing Companies (150 men and 30 M/T) attached to them for the servicing and light repair of aircraft. S.E.Fs. and short-range reconnaissance units have a similar body of men incorporated in their own establishments with extra M/T to make them as mobile as the rest of the unit.

Flying personnel fly their operational aircraft from the old to the new bases. But a general principle adopted in moves of flying units is for an advance party with selected ground personnel (including signals personnel) to be sent ahead by air transport.

APPENDIX E—continued.

The type of unit usually forming a basis for permanent moves is the Gruppe of 30 aircraft. S.E.F. and D.B. units often, however, move in the strength of two Gruppen at a time.

Smaller formations than a Gruppe are frequently moved both from rear areas to the front and from one base to another at the front. A unit undergoing re-equipment in Germany will often be despatched to the front in successive Staffeln of nine aircraft as they are brought up to strength. Conversely a Gruppe at the front may send back its Staffeln to Germany one by one for re-equipment. At the front, single Staffeln of nine aircraft may be detached from the Gruppe to a more advanced airfield for a period of operations, or sent to reinforce another Gruppe in the neighbourhood. During a rapid advance difficulties of airfield accommodation and supply often prescribe a piecemeal sending forward of one Staffel at a time to a newly acquired airfield.

On a moving battle-front short-range units naturally have to be prepared to move more frequently than long-range ones, and at shorter notice. In these conditions, a short-range unit will keep most of its stores and equipment loaded on its M/T.

Air transport for moves of flying units is provided by the Luftflotte or Fliegerkorps. The number of transport aircraft required depends not only on the type of unit, but on the distance and the degree of permanence of the move. For the move of a Gruppe it varies as widely as from 3 to 20 aircraft. Freight-carrying gliders are also used.

There have been instances of the whole personnel of a Gruppe being moved by air. Airfield Commands have been similarly transported. But these are exceptional occasions.

APPENDIX F

G.A.F. NAVAL CO-OPERATION

An Outline Classification of Types of Activity

1. The task of G.A.F. naval co-operation may be said to start with reconnaissance. The G.A.F. provides the long-range eyes of the Navy. Allied ships (Naval and other) are searched for and their positions reported to the German Naval Commands so that the targets may be attacked. Discovery is sometimes followed by shadowing in order that the subsequent movements of the prospective prey may also be reported.

2. Visual reconnaissance is often supplemented by photographic reconnaissance, especially where ships are in harbours and anchorages. The search for ships may be carried out by aircraft with special Radar equipment installed for that purpose.

3. The G.A.F. may also act as the eyes of the Navy in making reports of areas clear of hostile ships or of the positions of friendly ships. It sometimes undertakes search for ships which are overdue or thought to have been damaged. Furthermore, it provides the Navy with the results of meteorological reconnaissances and, in the extreme North, of ice reconnaissances.

4. Sometimes, however, the G.A.F. orders sorties with the object of targets at sea being attacked by the reconnoitring aircraft. In this way simple reconnaissance develops into offensive or armed reconnaissance. This kind of operation has for its objectives Naval ships, merchantmen, or submarines or all of them. A frequent area to be so covered is that of convoy routes.

5. It is not always necessary for an aircraft attacking shipping to have itself carried out previous reconnaissance. Suitable reconnaissance aircraft may have carried out a successful search preparatory to attack by bomber or torpedo aircraft which have been kept at readiness for the purpose. Alternatively, information of location may have been obtained from Naval or similar sources.

6. Some types of naval co-operation are purely offensive and do not require reconnaissance immediately preceding them, for instance mine-laying in enemy waters.

7. There is also reconnaissance which is essentially defensive. The aircraft carrying out this type of reconnaissance will only attack if the object of its protection is attacked or is liable to be attacked. This defence may take the form of patrols for the protection of ships in harbour or at anchor or of ships on the move, e.g. naval formations or convoys. The defence may be against surface ships, or submarines, or aircraft. For instance, fighter aircraft may be ordered to look out for and attack aircraft threatening U-Boats, or bomber aircraft may be ordered to provide flank reconnaissance for such operations as mine-laying.

8. Air escort of shipping may be regarded as a special form of defensive reconnaissance. The escort may be "close" (when the use of single-engine fighters is desirable) or "distant" (when longer range aircraft are used). If it is close, the task is chiefly that of watching for attacking aircraft and attempting to shoot them down or to make them sheer off. If the escort is distant, the reconnaissance aspect is more marked, as, for instance, in the case of an anti-submarine patrol in front of a German convoy. (These anti-submarine patrols will generally be by aircraft carrying bombs suitable for attacks on any submarines that may be sighted). The expressions "distant escort" and "flank reconnaissance" are sometimes used alternatively.

9. If a reconnaissance aircraft protecting a convoy or formation reports hostile surface ships likely to attack, the relevant G.A.F. Command may call into operation a torpedo aircraft staffel kept at readiness for that purpose. Essentially defensive reconnaissance may thus develop into the offensive.

10. The organisation of escort varies with the nature of the expected attacks and on the kind of area through which the protected ships are passing. If the course is a coastal one, the organisation of the escort will obviously be different from that over the open sea. In the former case, the use of relays of fighters may be more practicable.

11. There are types of naval co-operation which are purely defensive such as the laying of smoke screens by aircraft so as to protect ships from attack.

12. In order that naval co-operation may be efficiently carried out, the G.A.F. send air liaison officers to the headquarters of Naval Commands ashore, and, if necessary, to Naval formations afloat. Fighter Control Officers are also sent by the G.A.F. to undertake duties on ships having charge of convoys which are being protected by S.E.Fs. Conversely, Naval officers are sent to G.A.F. headquarters as liaison officers when circumstances so require.

13. There is, of course, direct communication between aircraft and surface ships; and communication by W/T is also possible between aircraft and submarines. As far as submarines are concerned, it is believed that the usual practice is for the aircraft to communicate with its base so that such messages may be passed to the submarine through Naval channels. In suitable circumstances, aircraft can make visual signals both to ships and to submarines and can indicate by pre-arranged movements the position, for instance, of a hostile aircraft which has been sighted.

APPENDIX G

EMPLOYMENT OF AIR TRANSPORT

1. Kinds of employment

(a) *Transport of supplies and equipment for units of the G.A.F.*—There is a constant traffic of this kind for urgent requirements. But the use of transport aircraft for carriage of fuel, ammunition and other supplies and also aircraft equipment and signals and M/T equipment may be much increased on battle-fronts where road and rail communications are inadequate, are in the course of being organised, or have broken down.

(b) *Transfer of operational units to new bases.*—It constantly happens that flying units have to be moved from one part of a front to another, or from front to front with the least possible delay. These transfers are carried out partly by transport aircraft. The amount of equipment and the proportion of personnel so moved depends on such circumstances as the period of the move and the facilities available at the destination (see Appendix E).

(c) *Transport of supplies for the Army.*—When the Army's system of transport of supplies has broken down, or is inadequate, or its spearheads have outrun the system, or when parts of the Army have been cut off or surrounded, transport aircraft come to the Army's assistance, presumably on the orders of the Supreme Command of the Armed Forces. On one or two occasions such assistance has been on a large scale. Over 800 transport aircraft of all types are thought to have been used at Stalingrad in January, 1943. The Army in North Africa was having frequent supplies delivered to it by air in the last two years of the campaign. Supplies are sometimes dropped by parachute.

(d) *Reinforcement and evacuation of Army personnel* when other means of transport are difficult or when part of the Army has been cut off or surrounded or when the Army's transport arrangements have broken down. The Army received reinforcements by air on many occasions in the Mediterranean, for instance in Crete, Tunisia, Sicily, Corsica, Sardinia and Croatia. About 200 transport aircraft, plus a number of gliders, were used to evacuate Army troops from the Kuban in February, 1943. Some 4,000 men a day were so transferred.

(e) *Evacuation of wounded, chiefly Army.*—There are a limited number of special ambulance transport aircraft; but all transport aircraft can be fitted with improvised stretcher supports. The bulk of casualties moved are accommodated in aircraft returning from the front after bringing up supplies or fresh troops.

(f) *Airborne operations, including dropping of parachutists and air-landing of troops either by aircraft or by gliders.*—During the period that transport aircraft are allocated for these activities they are under the operational control of an officer known as the Fliegerfuehrer of Fliegerkorps XI. There is naturally close co-operation between the specialist Fliegerkorps for Air Transport and Fliegerkorps XI.

(g) *Miscellaneous employment.*—There are Courier Staffeln of mixed types of aircraft for transporting officers, mail and despatches and for assisting in co-operation between the G.A.F. and the Army especially in regard to reconnaissance. There are also Liaison Staffeln used in connection with co-operation with the Army in regard to air support.

2. Types of aircraft

The Ju.52 which has been the standard type for many years is still the largest in number. Some of these are floatplanes. He.111s (now obsolescent for operational purposes) are being used for air transport, including dropping parachutists.

Ju.90s and Ju.290s are used in small numbers. Giant powered gliders (Me.323s) are being regularly used and carry ten tons compared with the two tons carried by the Ju.52. There is also a smaller powered glider, the Go.244. Miscellaneous types are used in Communications Staffeln, varying from Ju.52s and He.111s to Me.108s, F.W.58s, Fieseler 156s and W.34s.

Gliders for freight-carrying are of three main types:—
The D.F.S.230 for small cargoes, but chiefly for personnel, the Go.242 for heavier cargoes, and the giant Me.321 for very heavy cargoes. Tugs for gliders are:—

(i) Ju.52, Do.17, Avia and Hs.126 for D.F.S.230s.
(ii) Ju.52 and He.111 for Go.242s.
(iii) He.111Z (5-engined) for Me.321.

3. Types of freight

Besides personnel, freight carried for the G.A.F. includes fuel (for aircraft and M/T), bombs and ammunition, rations, miscellaneous supplies, aircraft equipment, signals and M/T equipment. For the Army are included fuel, ammunition, guns and other arms, small tanks, (dismantled) rations and clothing. M/T has regularly been moved by air in Me.323s and Me.321s.

INDEX OF MAIN SUBJECTS

Subject	Page
Air Ministry	54, 56
Air Parks	28, 54, 56, 58
Air Transport	42, 48, 50, 52, 73–4, 76
Aircraft, Provision and Maintenance of	54, 71
Airfield Commands	28, 30, 32, 34, 54, 56, 71, 73
Armies, Numbered, Positions of	2, 6, 12, 16, 20
Army, Air Transport for	48, 50, 52, 76
Army Co-operation	44
Balkan Campaign	10, 40
Centre, A.O.C. in C.	12, 26
Close Support for Army	44
Defence of Airfields	71, 73
Equipment, Aircraft, Provision of	56, 58, 71
Equipment, Director General of	54, 56
Equipment Depots in Germany	54, 56, 58
Equipment Group in Luftgau	28, 54, 56
Equipment Issuing Stations	56, 71, 73
Escort of Ships	75
Field Air Parks	56, 58
Fighter Protection for Army	44
Fighters in Naval Co-operation	46
Fliegerdivisions	2, 8, 10, 22
Fliegerfuehrers	10, 12, 14, 22, 46
Fliegerkorps, Functions of	66, 67–70
Fliegerkorps, Moves of	67–70
Fliegerkorps, Positions of	2–22, 67–70
Flying Units, Composition of	52, 73–4
Flying Units, Employment of	36, 38
Flying Units, Moves of	34, 40, 42, 67–69, 73
Flying Units, Re-equipment of	67–69
France, Battle of	6, 8
France, G.A.F. in	10, 12, 22, 30
Ground Organisation, in North Africa	34, 72
Liaison Officers, with Army	44
Liaison Officers, with Navy	75
Long-range Bombers	36, 73
Luftflotte Areas, in Germany	2, 24, 26, 67
Luftflotte Areas, in Occupied Countries	2–12, 30, 32, 67
Luftflotten, Fliegerkorps under	67–69, 70
Luftflotten, Functions of	2, 54, 66
Luftgau Staffs, Special	30, 32
Luftgaus, in Germany	24, 26, 28
Luftgaus, in Occupied Countries	26, 30, 32
Luftgaus, Functions of	54, 56, 66
Maintenance of Aircraft	54, 71
Mediterranean	10, 12, 14, 18, 34, 42, 48, 50
Naval Co-operation	46, 75
North Africa, Ground Organisation in	34, 72
Norway, G.A.F. in	6, 10, 69, 75
Norwegian Campaign	6
Polish Campaign	2, 4
Protection, Air, for Army	44
Reconnaissance, Air, for Army	44
Reconnaissance, Air, for Navy	46, 75
Russian Campaign	12–22, 32, 67–70
Short-Range Flying Units	38, 73
Signals Communications, in Army Co-operation	44, 60
Signals Communications, in Navy Co-operation	75
Signals Communications, on Airfields	60, 71
Signals Organisation	60
Strength of First-Line Aircraft	2–22, 34
Strength of Air Transport Aircraft	52
Strength, Personnel, in North Africa	34, 72
Support for Army	44
Supplies, Provision of	28, 56, 71
Training	52, 62, 64
Transport Aircraft	42, 48, 50, 52, 73–4, 76
Works Personnel on Airfields	71

BAOR
BATTLEFIELD TOUR GUIDES

You don't get much better than this for first-hand information from the officers who commanded the formations and units carrying out these operations, these collected before time had blurred their memories of events

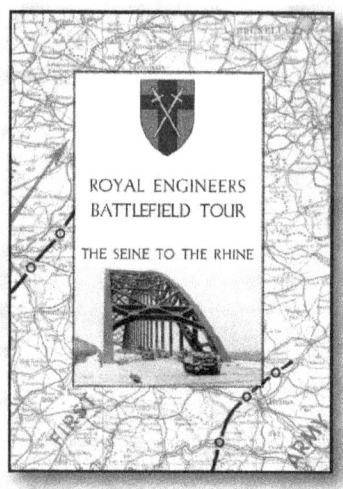

BAOR ROYAL ENGINEERS BATTLEFIELD TOUR
THE SEINE TO THE RHINE

Vol. 1 – An account of the operations included in the tour
Vol. 2 – A guide to the conduct of the tour

SB: 9781783316717
HB: 9781783317714

BAOR ROYAL ENGINEERS BATTLEFIELD TOUR
NORMANDY TO THE SEINE

SB: 9781783317516
HB: 9781783317813

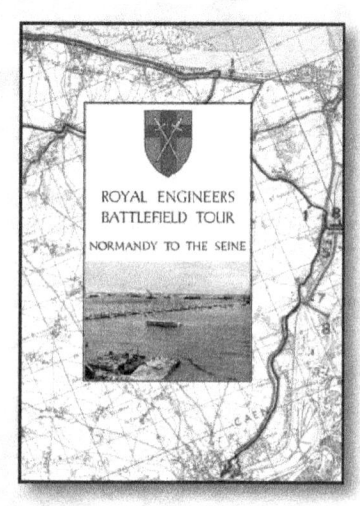

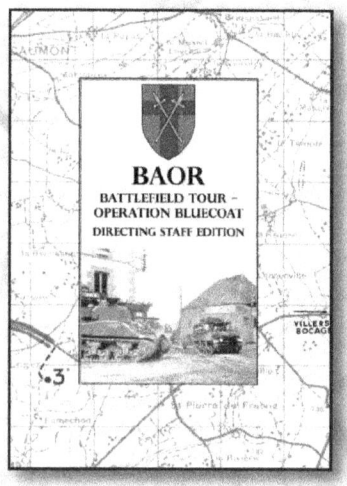

BAOR BATTLEFIELD TOUR
OPERATION BLUECOAT
– Directing Staff Edition

SB: 9781783318124
HB: 9781783318438

BAOR BATTLEFIELD TOUR
OPERATION VERITABLE
– Directing Staff Edition

SB: 9781783318131
HB: 9781783318421

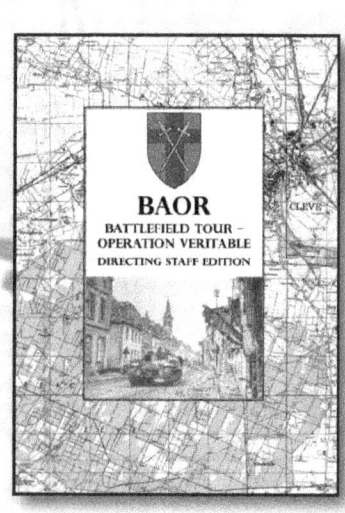

**BAOR BATTLEFIELD TOUR
OPERATION NEPTUNE**
– Spectators Edition
43(W) Division Assault Crossing of the River Seine
25-28 August 1944

SB: 9781474535298
HB: 9781474535311

**BAOR BATTLEFIELD TOUR
OPERATION PLUNDER**
– Directing Staff Edition

SB: 9781474535328
HB: 9781474535335

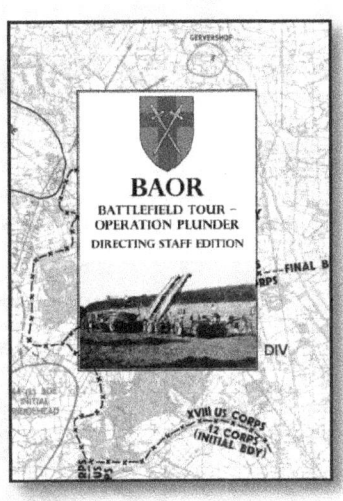

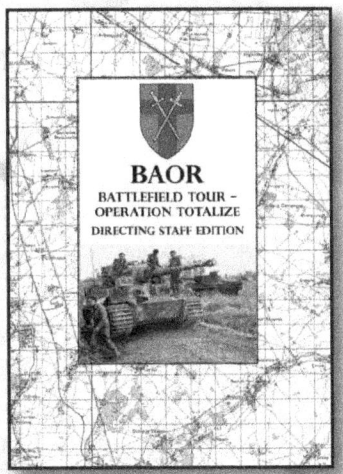

**BAOR BATTLEFIELD TOUR
OPERATION TOTALIZE**
– Directing Staff Edition

2 Canadian Corps Operations Astride the Road
Caen-Falaise 7-8 August 1944

SB: 9781474535342
HB: 9781474535359

**BAOR BATTLEFIELD TOUR
OPERATION VARSITY**
– Directing Staff Edition

Operations of XVIII Unites States Corps (Airborne) in
Support of the Crossing of the Rhine 24 & 25 March 1945

SB: 9781474535366
HB: 9781474535373